Dobermann

about pets

A guide to selection, care, nutrition, rearing, training, health, breeding, sports and play.

This book is an essential for every Dobermann owner or anyone considering a Dobermann as a pet.

P.O. Box 26, 9989 ZG Warffum, the Netherlands
www.aboutpets.info
E-mail: management@aboutpets.info

ISBN: 9789058218230

First edition 2009
Second edition: 2011

Photos: About Pets photography team

Breed information: Maya Brünner

Acknowledgements:
Photos: Cees and Tiny Konings, Heiko and Sabine Lorenz, Angela van Hoogstraten, Elly Elsenaar, Bert Kruisdijk, Annet van den Heuvel, Leonie Huitema
Anatomic illustrations: Hill's
Graphs: Courtesy of Royal Canin

Contents

Foreword

This book is an essential for every Dobermann owner or anyone considering the breed as a pet. It traces the ancestry of the Dobermann, explores the breed standard and some pros and cons of buying the breed. There is also important advice on feeding, as well as information on initial training and an introduction to reproduction. Finally, this book includes sections on day-to-day care, health and some breed-specific ailments.

In general

Introduction the Dobermann

The Dobermann is a muscular, medium-sized, powerfully built dog with a proud posture that has many enthusiasts across the world. He is not always the easiest dog for strangers to deal with, but his master and family mean everything to a Dobermann. This characteristic makes him not only a good pet and companion, but also an excellent working dog. His high level of intelligence helps him in any sport and ensures that life with a Dobermann is never boring.

Origins

Around 1870 the Dobermann was bred from several types of dogs (butcher's dogs [ancestors of the Rottweiler], ancestors of German Shepherds, German short haired Pinscher, short haired hunting dogs and several other kinds of dogs). The breed was created by Ferdinand Louis Dobermann from Apolda (Thüringen), who gave his own name to the breed. The so-called "butcher's dogs", which were already considered a relatively pure breed at that time, played the most important role in the development of the Dobermann breed. These dogs were an early type of Rottweiler, mixed with a type of shepherd dog, which existed in "Thüringen" as a black dog with rust red markings. Mr. Dobermann earned his living as a flayer, a dogcatcher, a policeman and as a bailiff. While he was doing his job, he always was accompanied by highly protective and obedient dogs. The people from Apolda called them Dobermannish dogs. From his breeding stock he crossed the most highly protective dogs with each other. His gray bitch "Schnuppe" became particularly well known. She was a cross of shorthaired Shepherd and Pinscher, and was crossed with the Butcher's Dogs (ancestors from the Rottweiler). In his breeding Mr. Dobermann also used mixes of Pinschers and Hunting-breeds. The Dobermann is the only German breed, which bears the name of his original breeder, Friedrich Louis Dobermann (02.01.1834 – 09.06.1894).

Thus he created "his breed" that was used as alert, and highly protective, working and housedogs. They were often used as guard and police dogs and used in hunting to control large vermin.

During the first years that the breed existed they were extremely highly protective dogs, which were prepared to attack the devil himself if necessary. An owner from those days, Gottfried Liechti said: '... one needed to have some courage when one wanted to own a dog like that.' This reputation of the breed lead him to the U.S.A. One of the first imported dogs immediately won three times Best in Show, before a judge had the nerves to look into his mouth and only saw that the dog was lacking several teeth, a big fault within this breed.

In 1894, after the death of Friedrich Louis Dobermann, the Germans named the breed Dobermann Pinscher in his honour. However, in the 1950's the Germans dropped the word Pinscher and so did the British people. In America the breed is still called Dobermann Pinscher.

The man who substantially continued to create this breed and took care of it was Mr. Otto Göller, who really made a major contribution to the Dobermann breed. Shortly after the turn of the century, his book 'Der Dobermannpinscher in Wort und Bild', was published. Mr. Otto Göller contributed quite a lot to the rapid and extensive spreading of the breed. In his 'Von Thüringen' kennels he continued breeding goal-orientated manner. He bought a lot of dogs from the area where he lived, he chose the dogs with whom he

wanted to breed and sold the descendants as far as Central and South America.

Gustav Krumbholz from the 'Ilm-Athen' kennels was also somebody who contributed a lot to this breed, together with Goswin Tischler from the 'Von Grönland' kennels. Goswin Tischler was the man who worked hard to get the breed recognized in 1895.

In 1889 the Dobermann was exhibited at a dog show for the first time. During a show of the Kynological Club Apolda, on 27th August 1899, the first Breeding Club was established with Otto Göller as its president. The club was called 'Dobermann-Pinscher-Klub Apolda'. One year later, in 1900, the name of the club was changed into 'Nationaler Dobermann-Pinscher-Klub für Deutschland e.V". Much later, when other Breeding Clubs were established, the Breeding Club from Apolda was called 'Urklub von 1899'. This first Dobermann Club did the work to get the breed accepted by the 'Delegierten Commission' (Delegates Commission). From 1899 onwards breeding only was done with certain breeding lines.

In 1900 the first Dobermann was registered in the German pedigree of the 'Delegierten Commission' and during the years afterwards one can see that the breed became more and more popular.
The 'Delegierten Commission' (DC) was established in 1879 and is thus the oldest canine organisation. However, from 20th July 1935 onwards it was forbidden and had to be abolished due to a decision of the "Geheimen Staatspolizeiamt" (secret national police service).

Because of the evils and hunger of World War I (1914 – 1918), many of the best Dobermanns were sold to the U.S.A, where many people supported this breed. Other Dobermanns were used by the army in World War I. and II. The U.S.A. used the Dobermann as a Marine War Dog. They were used by the army as sentries, messengers and scouts. In 1944 several Marine

War Dogs gave their lives while liberating Guam, 25 of these brave heroes were Dobermann Pinschers.

The first American Dobermann Pinscher Club was established in 1921. Much later, the Dobermann found his way to Great Britain as well. In 1933 the first Dobermann was exhibited at a British Dog Show.

As mentioned before, the initial goal of Louis Ferdinand Dobermann was to breed the perfect guard dog. The Dobermann breed still exemplifies "Guard Dog". According to literature, the first dogs were supposed to display aggressiveness and a bad temper. Improvements in breeding succeeded in creating a pleasant, affectionate and intelligent working dog. The Dobermann breed is a medium sized, powerful, muscular dog. Despite his substance, he should be elegant and noble, which will be evident in his bodyline. He must be exceptionally suitable as a companion, protection and working dog and also as a family dog.

Especially the dogs from the U.S. A., the U.K., the Netherlands, Germany and Switzerland as well as the Czech Republic and Hungary contributed to the high quality standard of the Dobermann breed.

The U.K. Working Group

According to the UK Kennel Club, the Dobermann belongs to the Working Group. This group consists of dogs that were selectively bred to become guards and search and rescue dogs. The dogs from the Working Group are the real specialists in their working fields; they excel in their type of work. It is said that the dogs belonging to the Working Group are some of the most heroic canines in the world; they help humans in many different ways. Some of the dogs that belong to this group are the Dobermann, the Great Dane, the Newfoundland, the St. Bernard and the Boxer.

The A.K.C. Working Group

According the A.K.C. the Dobermann Pinscher belongs to the Working Group. The dogs that belong to this group were bred to perform jobs as guarding property, pulling sleds and performing water rescues. Throughout the ages, these dogs were very valuable for the humans. Some of the breeds that belong to this group are the Doberman Pinscher, Siberian Husky, Newfoundland and Great Dane. As they all are quick learners, these intelligent and capable dogs became very trustworthy animals. Most of the dogs from this group have considerable dimensions and strength and this makes many working dogs unsuitable as a pet for the average family. And of course, only because of their size these dogs need to be properly trained.

Character

The disposition of the Dobermann is friendly and calm; very devoted to the family, he loves children. Medium temperament and medium sharpness (alertness) is desired. A medium threshold of irritation is required with a good contact to the owner. Easy to train, the Dobermann enjoys working, and shall have good working ability, courage and hardness. The particular values of self-confidence and intrepidness are required, and also adaptability and attention to fit the social environment.

Appearance

The Dobermann is of medium size, strong and muscularly built. Through the elegant lines of his body, his proud stature, and his expression of determination, he conforms to the ideal picture of dog.

UK Kennel Club and its breed standards

What does the UK Kennel Club do?

To say it in their own words: "The Kennel Club is committed to developing and supporting a nation of responsible dog owners. As well as organising events and campaigns to help dog owners meet their responsibilities, the Kennel Club also produces a range of literature to assist the dog owning public."

What is the use of a Breed Standard?

The Kennel Club explains that "the basis of breed shows is the judging of dogs against the 'Breed Standard', which is the prescribed blueprint of the particular breed of dog. For all licensed breed shows, the Kennel Club Breed Standards must be used for the judging of dogs."

More about the UK Kennel Club Breed Standards:
"The Breed Standards are owned by the Kennel Club, and all changes are subject to approval by the Kennel Club General Committee. New Breed Standards, for newly recognised breeds, are drawn up once the breed has become sufficiently established within the UK. Careful research is conducted into the historical background, health and temperament of any new breed before Kennel Club recognition is granted. The Kennel Club currently recognises 210 breeds. Upon recognition, breeds are placed on the Imported Breed Register until they are deemed eligible for transferral to the Breed Register".

A standard provides a guideline for breeders and judges. It is used as an ideal that dogs of each breed can be compared to in order to assess the quality of their breeding - breeders strive to meet this standard in their dogs. In some breeds, dogs have been bred that already reach this standard; other breeds have a long way to go. There is a list of defects for each breed; these can be serious defects that disqualify the dog, in which case it will be excluded from breeding. Permitted defects are not serious, but do cost points in a show. A standard has been developed for all breeds recognised by the FCI (Fédération Cynologique Internationale).

More about the FCI

The Fédération Cynologique Internationale is the World Canine Organisation. The FCI has 86 members all over the world and contract partners (one member per country); each country issues its own pedigrees and trains its own judges. The FCI makes sure that the pedigrees and judges are mutually recognised by all the FCI members. The FCI is the worldwide umbrella organisation in the dog world. The officially approved breed associations of the member countries provide translations of the breed standard.

The FCI recognises 341 breeds (2011), and each breed is the 'property' of a specific country. The country, which is 'owner' of the breed, writes the standard - a description of the ideal type - of this breed in co-operation with the Standards and Scientific Commissions of the FCI. The translation and updating are carried out by the FCI. The breed-standards are incredibly important as they act as the reference for judges when they judge dogs in shows held in the FCI member countries.
The breed-standard is also THE reference that assists the breeders in their attempt to produce top-quality dogs.

The UK Kennel Club Breed Standard for the Dobermann

General Appearance
Medium size, muscular and elegant, with well set body. Of proud carriage, compact and tough. Capable of great speed.

Characteristics
Intelligent and firm of character, loyal and obedient.

Temperament
Bold and alert. Shyness or viciousness very highly undesirable.

This visualisation is intended to help explain some of the terms used in the breed standard.

Head and Skull
In proportion to body. Long, well filled out under eyes and clean cut, with good depth of muzzle. Seen from above and side, resembles an elongated blunt wedge. Upper part of head flat and free from wrinkle. Top of skull flat, slight stop; muzzle line-extending parallel to top line of skull. Cheeks flat, lips tight. Nose solid black in black dogs, solid dark brown in brown dogs, solid dark grey in blue dogs and light brown in fawn dogs. Head out of balance in proportion to body, dish-faced, snipy or cheeky very highly undesirable.

Eyes
Almond-shaped, not round, moderately deep set, not prominent, with lively, alert expression. Iris of uniform colour, ranging from medium to darkest brown in black dogs, the darker shade being more desirable. In browns, blues, or fawns, colour of iris blends with that of markings, but not of lighter hue than markings; light eyes in black dogs highly undesirable.

Ears
Small, neat, set high on head. Normally dropped, but may be erect.

Mouth
Well developed, solid and strong with complete dentition and a perfect, regular and complete scissor bite, i.e. upper teeth closely overlapping lower teeth and set square to the jaws. Evenly placed teeth. Undershot, overshot or badly arranged teeth highly undesirable.

Neck
Fairly long and lean, carried with considerable nobility; slightly convex and in proportion to shape of dog. Region of nape very muscular. Dewlap and loose skin undesirable.

Forequarters
Shoulder blade and upper arm meet at an angle of 90 degrees. Shoulder blade and upper arm approximately equal in length. Short upper arm relative to shoulder blade highly undesirable. Legs seen from front and side, perfectly straight and parallel to each

other from elbow to pastern; muscled and sinewy, with round bone in proportion to body structure. Standing or gaiting, elbow lies close to brisket.

Body

Square, height measured vertically from ground to highest point at withers equal to length from fore chest to rear projection of upper thigh. Fore chest well developed. Back short and firm, with strong, straight topline sloping slightly from withers to croup; bitches may be slightly longer to loin. Ribs deep and well sprung, reaching to elbow. Belly fairly well tucked up. Long, weak, or roach backs highly undesirable.

Hindquarters

Legs parallel to each other and moderately wide apart. Pelvis falling away from spinal column at an angle of about 30 degrees. Croup well filled out. Hindquarters well developed and muscular; long, well bent stifle; hocks turning neither in nor out. When standing, hock to heel perpendicular to the ground.

Feet
Well arched, compact, and cat-like, turning neither in nor out. Long, flat deviating feet and/or weak pasterns highly undesirable.

Tail
Previously customarily docked.
Docked:
Docked at 1st or 2nd joint. Appears to be a continuation of spine without material drop.
Undocked:
Appears to be a continuation of spine without material drop, kink or deformity. May be raised and carried freely when the dog is moving or standing.

Gait/Movement
Elastic, free, balanced and vigorous, with good reach in forequarters and driving power in hindquarters. When trotting, should have strong rear drive, with apparent rotary motion of hindquarters. Rear and front legs thrown neither in nor out. Back remains strong and firm.

Coat
Smooth, short, hard, thick and close lying. Imperceptible undercoat on neck permissible. Hair forming a ridge on back of neck and/or along spine highly undesirable.

Colour
Definite black, brown, blue or fawn (Isabella) only, with rust red markings. Markings to be sharply defined, appearing above each eye, on muzzle, throat and fore chest, on all legs and feet and below tail. White markings of any kind highly undesirable.

Size
Ideal height at withers: dogs: 69 cms (27 ins); bitches: 65 cms (251/2 ins). Considerable deviation from this ideal undesirable.

Faults
Any departure from the foregoing points should be considered a fault and the seriousness with which the fault should be regarded should be in exact proportion to its degree and its effect upon the health and welfare of the dog and on the dog's ability to perform its traditional work.

Note
Male animals should have two apparently normal testicles fully descended into the scrotum.

U.K. Kennel Club Breed Standard, last update effective October 2009.

Reproduced by courtesy of The Kennel Club of Great Britain

NOTE:

Tails docked before the relevant dates

These dogs can continue to be shown at all shows in England, Wales, Scotland and Northern Ireland. However if the dog was docked on or around the various relevant dates (from 28th March 2007 to 30th April 2007 inclusive) one should refer to the detailed Questions and Answers as can be found on the website of the Kennel Club, which will describe the exact situation.

Tails docked on or after the relevant dates

Irrespective of where the dogs were docked, they may not be shown at shows in England and Wales where the public is charged a fee for admission. If the dogs were docked legally either in England, Wales, Northern Ireland or abroad they may be shown at any show in Scotland or Northern Ireland - but in England and Wales they may only be shown at shows where the public is admitted without the payment of a fee.
However if a dog was docked on or around the various relevant dates (from 28th March 2007 to 30th April 2007 inclusive) one should refer to the detailed Questions and Answers as can be found on the website of the Kennel Club, which will describe the exact situation.

More about the American Kennel Club

The American Kennel Club (A.K.C.) is the national kennel organisation of the United States. This organisation was already founded in 1884. The A.K.C. is not a member of the F.C.I.
The American Kennel Club is the national organisation for the registration of purebred dogs and they promote the sport of purebred dogs.
Apart from that the A.K.C. also promotes breeding purebred dogs for type and function. Furthermore the A.K.C. promotes responsible dog ownership and tries to protect the rights of all dog owners.
The A.K.C. tries to protect the health and well being of dogs.

The breed standards of the A.K.C. can differ from the F.C.I. and UK breed standards. Between the F.C.I. and the A.K.C. exists a letter of understanding in which several cooperation agreements are laid down.
Both organisations share the same common goals of promoting and protecting purebred dogs.

The American Kennel Club Breed Standard for the Dobermann Pinscher

In the U.S.A. the Dobermann Pinscher belongs to the Working Group.

General Appearance

The appearance is that of a dog of medium size, with a body that is square. Compactly built, muscular and powerful, for great endurance and speed. Elegant in appearance, of proud carriage, reflecting great nobility and temperament. Energetic, watchful, determined, alert, fearless, loyal and obedient.

Size, Proportion, Substance

Height at the withers: Dogs 26 to 28 inches, ideal about 27½ inches; Bitches 24 to 26 inches, ideal about 25½ inches. The height, measured vertically from the ground to the highest point of the withers, equalling the length measured horizontally from the fore chest to the rear projection of the upper thigh. Length of head, neck and legs in proportion to length and depth of body.

Head

Long and dry, resembling a blunt wedge in both frontal and profile views. When seen from the front, the head widens gradually toward the base of the ears in a practically unbroken line. Eyes almond shaped, moderately deep set, with vigorous, energetic expression. Iris, of uniform colour, ranging from medium to darkest brown in black dogs; in reds, blues, and fawns the colour of the iris blends with that of the markings, the darkest shade being preferable in every case. Ears normally cropped and carried erect. The upper attachment of the ear, when held erect, is on a level with the top of the skull. Top of skull flat, turning with slight stop to bridge of muzzle, with muzzle line extending parallel to top line of skull. Cheeks flat and muscular. Nose solid black on black dogs, dark brown on red ones, dark gray on blue ones, and dark tan on fawns. Lips lying close to jaws. Jaws full and powerful, well filled under the eyes.

Teeth strongly developed and white. Lower incisors upright and touching inside of upper incisors a true scissors bite. 42 correctly placed teeth, 22 in the lower, and 20 in the upper jaw. Distemper teeth shall not be penalized.
Disqualifying Faults: Overshot more than 3/16 of an inch. Undershot more than 1/8 of an inch. Four or more missing teeth.

Neck, Topline, Body

Neck proudly carried, well muscled and dry. Well arched, with nape of neck widening gradually toward body. Length of neck proportioned to body and head. Withers pronounced and forming the highest point of the body. Back short, firm, of sufficient width, and muscular at the loins, extending in a straight line from withers to the slightly rounded croup.
Chest broad with fore chest well defined. Ribs well sprung from the spine, but flattened in lower end to permit elbow clearance. Brisket reaching deep to the elbow. Belly well tucked up, extending in a curved line from the brisket. Loins wide and muscled. Hips broad and in proportion to body, breadth of hips being approximately equal to breadth of body at rib cage and shoulders.
Tail docked at approximately second joint, appears to be a continuation of the spine, and is carried only slightly above the horizontal when the dog is alert.

Forequarters

Shoulder Blade - sloping forward and downward at a 45-degree angle to the ground meets the upper arm at an angle of 90 degrees. Length of shoulder blade and upper arm are equal. Height from elbow to withers approximately equals height from ground to elbow. Legs seen from front and side, perfectly straight and parallel to each other from elbow to pastern; muscled and sinewy, with heavy bone. In normal pose and when gaiting, the elbows lie close to the brisket. Pasterns firm and almost perpendicular to the ground. Dewclaws may be removed. Feet well arched, compact, and catlike, turning neither in nor out.

Hindquarters

The angulation of the hindquarters balances that of the forequarters. Hip Bone falls away from spinal column at an angle of about 30 degrees, producing a slightly rounded, well filled-out croup. Upper Shanks at right angles to the hipbones are long, wide, and well muscled on both sides of thigh, with clearly defined stifles. Upper and lower shanks are of equal length. While the dog is at rest, hock to heel is perpendicular to the ground. Viewed from the rear, the legs are straight, parallel to each other, and wide enough apart to fit in with a properly built body. Dewclaws, if any, are generally removed. Cat feet as on front legs, turning neither in nor out.

Coat

Smooth-haired, short, hard, thick and close lying. Invisible gray undercoat on neck permissible.

Colour and Markings

Allowed Colours: Black, red, blue, and fawn (Isabella). Markings: Rust, sharply defined, appearing above each eye and on muzzle, throat and fore chest, on all legs and feet, and below tail. White patch on chest, not exceeding ½ square inch, permissible.
Disqualifying Fault: Dogs not of an allowed colour.

Gait

Free, balanced, and vigorous, with good reach in the forequarters and good driving power in the hindquarters. When trotting, there is strong rear-action drive. Each rear leg moves in line with the foreleg on the same side. Rear and front legs are thrown neither in nor out. Back remains strong and firm. When moving at a fast trot, a properly built dog will single-track.

Temperament

Energetic, watchful, determined, alert, fearless, loyal and obedient.
The judge shall dismiss from the ring any shy or vicious Doberman.
Shyness: A dog shall be judged fundamentally shy if, refusing to stand for examination, it shrinks away from the judge; if it fears an approach from the rear; if it shies at sudden and unusual noises to a marked degree.
Viciousness: A dog that attacks or attempts to attack either the judge or its handler, is definitely vicious. An aggressive or belligerent attitude towards other dogs shall not be deemed viciousness.

Faults

The foregoing description is that of the ideal Doberman Pinscher. Any deviation from the above-described dog must be penalized to the extent of the deviation.

Disqualifications

Overshot more than 3/16 of an inch, undershot more than 1/8 of an inch. Four or more missing teeth.
Dogs not of an allowed colour.

Approved February 6, 1982.
Reformatted November 6, 1990.

Reproduced by courtesy of the American Kennel Club.

Purchase

If, after careful consideration, you have decided to buy a Dobermann, there are a number of options available to you. Do you want a puppy or an adult dog? Should it be a male or female?

One of the biggest questions that will arise, of course, is where you should buy your dog. Should you buy it privately or from a reliable breeder? For your own and the animal's sake, a few things should be decided in advance. After all, you want a dog that suits your situation and lifestyle.

Pros and cons of the Dobermann

As you have already read, the Dobermann is a nice companion, strongly focussed on his master. If he gets enough exercise, he will be very calm at home. His body is built for action and a walk around the block three times a day is definitely not enough. Besides being let out regularly, a Dobermann needs a good run for at least one hour per day. Anything more is very welcome. Build a puppy up to this very gradually. His bones still consist partly of soft cartilage and can quickly become deformed if overloaded. Even if you love to be out with your puppy all day, remember that you have his whole lifetime ahead of you to go for stiff walks with him. Try to provide variety during your walks. Hide a ball and get your dog to search for it, or jog together. This variety will keep your Dobermann's mind active (something that is often forgotten).

Many people think of Dobermanns only as frightening guard dogs behind a fence. Sadly, some people consciously choose the breed because of that image, without thinking of other aspects. Choosing a Dobermann (or any other breed) that way is disastrous. Of course, the Dobermann was originally bred to be a watchdog, but he is far more than just that! He is a courageous and persevering dog that is used to taking matters into his own hands and, if he has to, taking care of his own well-being.

These characteristics make the Dobermann unique, but also mean that he is not a dog that will suit everybody. A Dobermann needs a lot of exercise and can be very dominant. He can also be a nuisance at times because, with his intelligence, he can happily solve "problems" on his own. The Dobermann therefore needs a strong, rigorous master who can give him what his history demands.

Male or female?

Whether you buy a male or a female is mainly a question of personal preference. Both can grow up to become attractive and well behaved members of the family. As far as working capacity is concerned, there is no difference between a dog and a bitch.

Males sometimes appear to be more self-assured and can display dominant behaviour, trying to play boss over other dogs, especially over other males, and, if they get the chance, over humans too. In the wild the most dominant dog (or wolf) was always the leader of the pack - and in most cases this was a male.
It is essential, in order to establish a good relationship between dog and owner, that the dog understands from the outset that you are the leader of the pack. This demands an understanding yet consistent upbringing.

Bitches usually become fertile (go on heat) between eight and twelve months. This happens twice a year and lasts two to three weeks. During the fertile period, especially during the second half of the season, the female will try to go out in search of a male to mate with. It is essential that you take precautions to prevent unwanted additions to the family.

A male will display more masculine behaviour once he becomes sexually mature. He will make clear to other dogs which territory is his by urinating frequently and in as many places as possible. He will also be very difficult to confine when there is a bitch in season in the area. However, as far as general care is concerned, there is little difference between male and female on a daily basis.

A puppy test is good way of determining what kind of character a young dog will develop. During this test you will usually notice that a dog is more dominant than a bitch; it is also often possible to quickly recognise the bossy, the adventurous and the cautious characters. Visit the litter a couple of times early on and try to pick a puppy that suits your own personality. A dominant dog, for instance, needs a strong hand as it will often try and test its boundaries. You must regularly make it clear who's the boss, and ensure that he understands he must obey all the members of the family.

Puppy or adult dog?

After you have decided you want a male or female, the question arises as to whether it should be a puppy or an adult dog?
Of course, it is great having a sweet little puppy in the house, but training a young dog requires a lot of time. In the first year it learns more than during the rest of its life. This is the period when the foundations are laid for fundamental training such as house-training, obedience and social behaviour. You should be prepared to devote a lot of time to training and caring for your puppy, especially in the first few months.

A puppy will no doubt leave a trail of destruction in its wake for the first few months, this will usually cost you a number of rolls of wallpaper, some good shoes and a few socks, in the worst case scenario you'll be left with some chewed furniture - though some puppies even manage to tear curtains from their rails! With some basic training this 'vandalism' will quickly disappear as your puppy grows.
The greatest advantage of a puppy is of course, that you can train it in your own way. The training a dog gets or does not get is a major influence on its whole character.

Training

A puppy requires a good deal of time and energy, but ultimately, you will have a significant influence on its character and behaviour, and will hopefully end up with a dog that suits you and your lifestyle.

Choosing an adult Dobermann is an option if training a puppy does not appeal to you. However, it is important to recognize that an older dog will still require a significant amount of input from you. An adult Dobermann is also likely to have developed its own habits, traits and characteristics that you will have to accept if you decide to choose an older dog. Equally, it will have probably grown used to a certain type of lifestyle, which you may struggle to adapt to.

Integrating an adult dog into a household with an existing dog can be tricky, and it is essential you handle this introduction with sensitivity. Both dogs will need time to adjust and establish their natural hierarchy.

If you are interested in an adult Dobermann you may want to consider rehoming a rescue dog. Most rescue dogs are older dogs in need of a new home through no fault of their own (e.g. a family breakdown or bereavement). However, it is important to be aware that you may experience some difficulties as you and the dog adjust to each other.

With experience and patience adopting a rescue dog is still a major task, as you may need to correct behavioural issues. Owning any dog is a pleasure for both owner and dog if you can establish a sound relationship.

Adopting a rescued Dobermann is by no means the easy option and you must be prepared to be vetted by the organization to ensure you are the right match for the dog in question. Most rescue centres will also ask for a donation to help cover the cost of caring for the dog - so it is not always the cheapest option either!

Two dogs?

Having two or more dogs can be great fun for both humans and dogs alike. As pack animals dogs really enjoy each other's company. If you are sure you want two young dogs, it is best not to buy them at the same time. Training a dog and establishing the bond between you and him takes time, and you need to give a lot of attention to the dog

in this phase - two puppies in the house means you have to divide your attention. Equally, there is a chance that they will focus on one another rather than on their owner.

It is best to buy a second pup when the first is an adult; two adult dogs can happily be brought into the household together and introducing a puppy when the first dog has matured often has a positive effect on the older dog. The influence of the puppy seems almost to give it a second puppyhood and the older dog, if it has been well trained, can help with the socialisation of the puppy, as young dogs like to imitate the behaviour of their elders. However it is important you divide your attention equally between both dogs. Take the puppy out alone at least once per day during the first eighteen months, and ensure both dogs get enough peace and quiet. You may have to physically separate Dobermann after a romp, as they never tire of playing together!

It is inadvisable to keep two male Dobermanns together. Male Dobermanns are too dominant to live together. For the first eighteen months they will pretend that everything is fine. But just when you lean back satisfied, because you think that you have succeeded after all, they attack each other and can no longer be kept in the same room.

The combination of an unneutered male and female also needs special attention as if you do not plan to breed with your dogs, you must take precautionary measures to prevent them mating when the bitch is in season. Spaying the bitch or neutering the male is essential if you are keeping a Dobermann as a pet.

The Dobermann and children

Dogs and children can be fantastic playmates, and children can learn important lessons in developing respect and a sense of responsibility through caring for a dog, or other pet. You can encourage this by including your child in the dog's day-to-day care. It is essential that the child understands that a dog is a living being and not a toy, as even the sweetest dog will express its unhappiness if it is being annoyed, and can become frightened, timid and even aggressive. Look for ways the child can play with the dog – games like hide-and-seek (where the child hides and the dog has to find it) are great in establishing a healthy fun-filled relationship between dog and child. While most dogs love playing with children, they do need quiet 'down' time where they are left in peace, and it is essential that you and your children learn to recognise and

accept when your dog has had enough. It can be helpful to create a quiet place for your dog to retreat to in the house when it wants some space - a crate or an indoor kennel can be useful here - especially when the dog is still growing and needs regular periods of rest.

The arrival of a baby can also create huge changes in the life of your dog. Before the birth you can help the dog get acquainted with the new situation by letting him sniff the new things in the house. When the baby has arrived involve the dog as much as possible in everyday life, but make sure it gets plenty of attention too.
NEVER leave a dog alone with young children. Crawling infants sometimes make unexpected movements, which can easily frighten a dog. Infants are hugely curious, and may irritate the dog by pulling his tail or invading his space while he is sleeping. Dogs, like all animals, are unpredictable, and even the most mild -mannered dog can instinctively defend itself when if it feels threatened.

A Dobermann and cats

Contrary to popular belief dogs and cats can coexist quite happily. It is important that you take the time to gently introduce a new puppy to the family cat. As long you ensure the cat has safe places to escape to, and separate places to eat and sleep, they should get along fine.
Many dogs will initially attempt to chase cats, and it is essential you stop this immediately, before it becomes a habit. As their body language is quite different, they need to learn from their experience. For example, a dog lying on its back is submissive.

A cat lying on its back is not at all submissive, but makes sure that it has its best weapons of defence, i.e. its claws, at its disposal. However, dogs and cats have one thing in common: they growl when they are angry, and both animals understand this. As far as nutrients are concerned, Dogs and cats must not share each other's food considering the nutrients. Dog food lacks a sufficient level of taurine, which is essential for cats. Dogs and cats must also not share a food bowl, as a dog will not tolerate another animal sharing its bowl. A persistent kitten might therefore get a serious ticking off from your dog. Playing together is fine, but you must prevent your pets eating together.
Some dogs (this is not a characteristic of any particular breed) love to eat cat faeces (coprophagia). To prevent your dog eating from the cat litter, place the litter box in another room, where only your cat has access, or place the litter box between two pieces of furniture to prevent your dog gaining access.

Where to buy your dog

The best and safest way of buying a puppy is through a reputable breeder, who you can find by contacting a breed club. Most breed clubs will not allow any breeder who has not carried out the necessary clearances of hip, elbows and eyes to be placed on their puppy register. Equally, The Kennel Club and American Kennel Club also run a puppy referral service on their websites, and help to place adult dogs that can no longer be kept by their owners due to personal circumstances.
Before choosing your breeder ensure you ask plenty of questions and visit several different kennels to gain an insight into the conditions the puppies are kept in.
Occasionally an owner of a pet Dobermann may decide to breed a litter of puppies. Hopefully the owner of the stud dog will have helped to advise the novice breeder on the importance of carrying out the necessary health checks, such as eye tests and hip and elbow scoring. It is essential that you ensure that both the dam and the sire of the litter have been tested thoroughly before buying a puppy.
Although you may be lucky and end up with the puppy of your dreams from a pet breeder, the lack of an established breeding line means that in reality the chances of getting exactly what you are looking for are much slimmer than if you seek advice from a recommended breeder in your area.
In general it is advisable to be extremely wary of puppies advertised in local papers. These may well be bred by so called

'puppy farmers' who breed for purely financial reasons and give little thought to the quality of the animals they are breeding from. Puppy farmers can rarely produce evidence for the recommended health checks and the bitch is often bred from season after season. This will continue until she is unable to produce any more litters, where upon she will be discarded - with little thought to her quality of life. Equally, puppies reared in this way can be of questionable temperament, and you will generally be unable to meet the parents of the litter.
Puppy farmers will often register the litter with the Kennel Club to make the puppies more saleable. Registration itself does not guarantee the legitimacy of the breeder and it is not a benchmark of quality. Buying a puppy from this type of breeder is a huge gamble and it is strongly advised you steer clear from anyone breeding dogs in this way.
Fortunately there are also enough responsible breeders with a good reputation. Ask if the breeder is prepared to help you after you have bought the puppy and to help you find solutions to questions or problems that may arise later on. Also, reputable breeders are aware of possible health disorders that are specific to certain breeds and the measures they may have taken in their breeding lines. Please read more on this subject in the Health chapter of this book.

Finally, you must also realise that a pedigree is nothing more or less than evidence of descent. A pedigree says nothing about the health of the parent dogs and the puppies.

Things to watch out for
Buying a puppy is a huge responsibility, and there is a lot to consider. Here is a checklist to help you make the right choice:

- Never buy a puppy on an impulse, even if it is love at first sight. A dog is a living being that will need a lot of care and attention over its long life. It is not a toy that you can ignore or grow tired of. By buying a puppy you are taking on a huge responsibility, but you will be rewarded by a love and companionship over many happy years!
- Take a good look at the mother. Is she calm, nervous, aggressive, well cared-for or neglected? The behaviour and condition of the mother is not only a sign of the quality of the breeder, but also of the puppy you are about to buy.
- Avoid buying a puppy whose mother appears to have little contact with humans. A young dog needs as many stimuli and experiences as possible during its early months. Exposure to the breeder's family means it can get used to humans, other pets and different sights and sounds. Kennel dogs miss these experiences and have often not been sufficiently socialised.
- Always ask to see the papers of the parents (vaccination certificates, pedigrees, official reports on health examinations such as hip- and eye-checks).
- Check whether the pups have been vaccinated and wormed. It is important you have a written record of any treatment administered to your puppy that you will be able to show your vet.
- Never buy a puppy younger than eight weeks.

* Put any agreement with the breeder in writing. A model agreement is available from the Kennel Club or from the Breed Club.

Ten golden puppy rules

1. Walk your puppy for no more than 20 minutes, followed by a short play, and then some hours sleep.
2. Never let a puppy run endlessly after a ball.
3. Do not let your puppy romp with large, heavy dogs.
4. Do not let your puppy play on a full stomach.
5. Never feed your puppy immediately after exercise.
6. Do not let your puppy go up and down the stairs in its first year. Also be careful with smooth floors.
7. Never add supplements to complete dog food.
8. Watch you puppy's weight. Being overweight can lead to many health problems.
9. Give your puppy a quiet place to sleep.
10. Pick up your puppy carefully, one hand under its chest and the other hand under its hindquarters.

Shopping list

- Collar
- Lead
- ID tag
- Blanket
- Water bowl
- Food bowl
- Poop scoop
- Food
- Comb
- Brush
- Toys
- Dog basket
- Indoor kennel/ crate

Travelling

Travelling with a dog is not always fun. Some dogs love a trip in the car, while others need a lot of coaxing even to get them in! Dogs can also suffer from carsickness, and if you are planning a holiday and want to take your dog with you, you should spend time getting them used to journeys.

That very first trip

The first trip of a puppy's life - from the breeder to its new home - is also the most nerve-wracking. If possible, pick up your puppy in the early morning, as this will give him the whole day to get used to his new environment. Ask the breeder not to feed your puppy on that day to avoid stomach upsets or carsickness en route home. Your puppy will be overwhelmed by all the new experiences and by leaving his mother and littermates. It has to go into a small space (the car) with all its new smells, noises and strange people. So there is a big chance that the puppy will be carsick this first time, with the possible consequence that it will remember travelling in the car as an unpleasant experience.

So it is important to make this first trip as pleasant as possible. When picking up a puppy, always take someone with you who can sit on the back seat with the puppy on his or her lap and talk to it calmly. It can happen that the puppy, in its nervousness, may urinate or be sick, so it is useful to take an old towel in the car.

Ask the breeder for a cloth or something else from the puppies' basket or bed that carries a familiar scent. The puppy can lie on this in the car, and this will also help if it feels lonely during the first nights at home. If the trip home is a long one, then stop for a break once in a while.
Let your puppy roam and sniff around on the lead providing the area is free of other dogs. Offer it something to drink and, if necessary, let it go to the toilet. It is also good advice to give a puppy positive experiences with car journeys. Make short trips to places where you can walk and play with it. After all, once in a while you will have to take your dog to certain places, such as to the veterinarian or to visit friends or acquaintances.

Carsickness

Walking a dog on the beach or in the woods is a good way to escape from the stress of day-by-day life - and dogs love it too! Often the first stage is a trip in the car. Most dogs have absolutely no problem with travelling, but some suffer from carsickness.

Many puppies suffer from nausea and vomiting on their first journey to their new home. The combination of fear and the car's motion plays a major role here and most puppies are only sick on this one occasion. However, for some dogs travel sickness can be a life-long problem and they can suffer terribly. If your Dobermann continues to suffer beyond its early puppyhood consult a vet about possible medication for this. The best way to get a puppy used to the car is to make lots of very short trips at first, with the puppy safely secured in a travel crate. It is very important that the puppy goes for a walk first and has had nothing to eat for four or five hours. Ensure the journey ends with a good destination, such as the woods, so your puppy associates the car with positive

experiences. If things go well, reward your puppy and then drive quietly home again. Never punish your dog if it whines or vomits during a car journey. The best thing is to pay no attention to it.
NEVER drag your dog into the car on its lead, instead coax it using positive reinforcement. If these short journeys go well, slowly build up the distance. It is also important to adjust your driving style where possible. Try and maintain a steady speed with no sudden braking, strong acceleration or sharp cornering.

Taking your Dobermann on holiday

When making holiday plans you will need to consider what you will do with your Dobermann. Are you taking it with you, putting it into a boarding kennel or leaving it with friends? What ever you decide will involve extra thought and planning in advance. If you choose to holiday with your dog, you need to be sure he will be welcome at your holiday home. If you are in the UK and going abroad it will need certain vaccinations and a health certificate, which normally needs to be done four weeks before departure. You must also be sure that you have made all the arrangements necessary to bring your dog back home without it needing to go into quarantine under the rabies regulations. Your vet can give you the most recent information. If your trip goes to southern Europe, ask for a treatment against ticks (you can read more about this in the chapter on parasites).

Although taking your dog on holiday can be part of the joy of ownership, you must seriously ask yourself if the dog is going to enjoy it as well. Dobermanns might suffer in hot countries and long days spent travelling in a car is equally unpleasant for many dogs. If you do decide to take your dog with you, make regular stops at safe places during your journey, so that your dog can have a good run, take plenty of fresh drinking water with you, as well as a good supply of your dog's usual diet. Never leave your dog in the car when the sun is shining. The temperature can quickly climb, leaving the dog in an awful and life-threatening situation. If you cannot avoid it, park the car in the shade and leave a window open for a little fresh air. Even if you have taken these precautions, frequently check on your dog and never stay away longer than is strictly necessary.

If you are travelling by plane or ship, leave plenty of time to make the necessary arrangements for your dog before you travel and investigate fully the rules that need to be observed. If you decide not to take your dog with you, you must find a place for him to stay while you are away. There are special boarding kennels for Dobermanns, but it is essential you book in advance, especially during busy summer holiday months. The kennel may also require certain vaccinations, which need to be given at least one month before the stay.

You may decide to employ a 'dog sitter' to come and stay in your own house and care for your dog. This also needs to be arranged well in advance and you must allocate time before you leave for the sitter to become acquainted with your dog and his routine. Always ensure that your dog can be traced in case it should run away or get lost while you are on holiday. A tag with home and holiday address and a mobile telephone number can prevent a lot of problems.

Moving home

Dogs are generally more attached to the humans they live with than to the house they live in. Moving home is usually not a problem for them, but it can be useful before moving to familiarise your dog with his new home and the surrounding area.

It is a good idea to leave your dog with relatives or friends or in a boarding kennel on the day of the move; this will reduce the chances of your dog becoming confused and getting lost during the stress of the move. When your move is complete, you can pick your dog up and let him settle quietly into his new home. Make sure you set up his bed immediately so he has somewhere familiar to go to in the new home.

During the first week or so, always walk your dog on a lead, because an animal can also get lost in new surroundings, and take different routes so he quickly gets to know the neighbourhood.

Do not forget to get your new address and phone number engraved on the dog's tag. Send a change of address notice to the institution that has the microchip data.

Feeding

A dog's diet actually consists of a lot more than just meat. In the wild it would eat its prey complete with skin and fur, including the bones, stomach and intestines with semi-digested vegetable material. In this way the dog would supplement its meat menu with the vitamins and minerals it needs. This is also the basis for feeding a domestic dog.

Basic principles of dog food

In general

Dogs have always been primarily carnivores (meat eaters). However, in the wild a minor part of their daily diet consisted of vegetable material or the vegetable-based content of their prey's stomach and intestines. In the past, dogs kept as pets used to be fed the remains of the family dinner.

Today, most dogs are fed a diet of dry or canned food, and over the last fifteen years, the diets of our domestic dogs and cats have changed hugely. There has been a marked advance in expertise and the foodstuffs have become increasingly sophisticated. To fully understand the effects of the foods available, it is important to have some understanding of the anatomy and physiology of dogs.

Anatomy and physiology of the dog's digestive tract

Ingested food first passes into the mouth, where it is crunched; dogs have no lateral movement in their jaws and therefore cannot chew, but during this crunching, the food is broken down into smaller pieces and moistened with saliva. The dog's saliva does not include digestive enzymes, so true digestion does not begin in the mouth. After swallowing, the food passes through the oesophagus to the stomach, where it is mixed and kneaded with gastric acid, i.e. one of the digestive juices. The gastric acid breaks down the proteins present in the food and kills off a large number of potentially harmful microorganisms, which are also present.

Once the food pulp has been kneaded through thoroughly and fulfils a number of chemical requirements, the closing muscle (pylorus) of the stomach relaxes and the food passes through into the duodenum.

The duodenum is the first part of the small intestine; here important digestive juices such as gall and the pancreatic juices are added to the food pulp. The gall juices help with the digestion of fat and the pancreatic juices contain enzymes, which help with the digestion of carbohydrates, proteins and fat. Enzymes are substances which are produced by the animal itself and which help with chemical transformation during digestion. The small intestine can be divided into three parts; the jejunum, ileum and caecum (appendix). The wall of the small intestine contains cells which provide the digestive juices, this wall has plenty of folds to provide as large a surface area as possible, where bacteria, which help in the digestive processes, and enzymes find a place to attach to. The actual digestion occurs in the small intestine and the foodstuffs are cut down into tiny pieces, which can be absorbed.

After being absorbed by the cells in the intestines, the nutrients are passed on to the blood, which transports the nutrients to the liver. The liver functions as a sort of traffic agent, which decides what needs to happen to the different nutrients and then sends them to the right place.

The large intestine (colon) follows on from the small intestine. The most important function here is to absorb the water from the food pulp. The intestine ends in the closing muscle (anus) via the rectum.

Food

Food contains many nutrients, which can be divided into six important groups: proteins, fats, carbohydrates, minerals, vitamins and water. Life cannot exist without water, but water does not actually contain any extra nutrients - unless it is mineral water, which can be very rich in certain minerals.

Proteins

Proteins look like a pearl necklace, consisting of different amino acids (the pearls). The amount and type of amino acids determines the characteristics of the protein in question.
The presence of nitrogen in all amino acids is important for the development of tissue.

Proteins fulfil many functions in the body; they are the most important components of tissue, hormones and enzymes.
Furthermore, they are responsible for maintaining water levels in the body, removing toxins and maintaining a good defence system.
Proteins are found in both vegetable (grains, legumes, yeast) and animal (meat, fish, poultry, eggs) form. An adult dog must have at least (20g protein/1000kcal food) 8% protein in the dry matter of its food (NRC 1985; NRC 2006) to maintain its health. In fact, if you want to ensure optimum health, maximum performance and good appearance, this percentage must be higher.

The story that protein is bad for dogs has long been disregarded as a myth. This was based on research carried out on rats, but at the end of the 1970s, research showed that the kidney metabolism of dogs is by no means as sensitive as that of rats. Since 1993, we also know that proteins do not have a detrimental impact on growth.

On the contrary, proteins, together with the right exercise, contribute to healthy muscles, which in turn stabilise the skeleton. This is a very important consideration for such conditions as hip dysplasia, for example. Proteins are a vital part of a healthy dog's diet, and a shortage of proteins will lead to anaemia, low resistance to illness, loss of muscle tissue, etc. A shortage of proteins is caused not only by insufficient absorption, but also through increased breakdown of proteins, which may be caused by many forms of stress (mental or physical strain on the individual animal).
An influence of protein on behaviour is not yet clear.

Fat

The most important function of fats is to provide energy. Fats also provide unsaturated fatty acids, which fulfil important functions in the nervous systems and the skin's metabolism. In general fats in the food are very easily digested by dogs; they can digest as much as 95 - 98%. Dogs, like humans, prefer food with a higher fat content, which is why it is often added to dog food to make it 'tastier'. Fat is also important as it stores some vitamins.

Carbohydrates

Carbohydrates (such as starch and sugar) always originate in vegetable material. You can differentiate between digestible carbohydrates (starch, simple sugars) and non-digestible carbohydrates (cellulose, pectin), which come from the cell membranes and fibres of plants. Carbohydrates improve the transport of the food pulp in the intestines by stimulating the membrane of the intestines, this in turn, stimulates the peristaltic movement of the intestines. A disadvantage of carbohydrates is that they increase the volume of the faeces, as they also hold a lot of water. Fibres are a good compromise as they perform a similar function throughout the major part of the intestines, and are then broken down at the last stage by bacteria in the large intestine. Fibres are broken down into substances, which partly function as a source of food for the cells of the large intestine, beet pulp, for example, contains these valuable fibres.

Minerals

Minerals, in terms of the amount consumed, only play a minor role in your dog's diet, but nonetheless they are absolutely vital. As minerals are only needed in such small amounts, mistakes are easily made. Minerals are divided into macro-minerals and micro-minerals or trace elements. Calcium (Ca) and phosphorus (P) are well-known macro-minerals; they play an important part in building up the skeleton and, depending on the physiological phase, must be provided in the diet in a fixed relation to each other.
Other important macro-elements include: magnesium (Mg) (skeleton, enzymes), sodium (Na), potassium (K) and chlorine (Cl). Some examples of micro-minerals include: iron (Fe) (blood, oxygen transport), copper (Cu) (creation of pigment, blood), zinc (Zn) (enzymes, skin), manganese (Mn) (enzymes), iodine (I) (thyroid hormone) and selenium (Se) (muscle tissue, anti-oxidant).

Vitamins

Vitamins can be of both vegetable and animal origins. Vitamins are divided into two groups - water-soluble and non-water-soluble. Vitamins are also required in only very small amounts, and dogs are able to produce a number of vitamins themselves. Below, we will list a number of important vitamins and their functions.

Some important functions of vitamins

	function	shortage	excess
vitamin A	fertility, skin and eyes	fertility problems, night blindness	abnormal bone metabolism vitamin K deficiency
vitamin D3	bone metabolism	abnormal bone metabolism	abnormal bone metabolism, kidney malfunction
vitamin E	with Se protection, muscle cells, anti-oxidant	fertility problems, muscle dystrophy	
vitamin K	blood clotting	haemorrhages	
vitamin C	collagen metabolism, resistance, mucous membranes	connective tissue damage, haemorrhages, liver necrosis	
B1 (thimaine)	carbohydrate metabolism, nervous system	anorexia, circulation problems, diarrhoea, atrophic reproductive organs	
B2 (riboflavine)	catalyst, energy production, protein metabolism	anorexia, growth delays, circulation problems	
PP (niacine)	catalyst, resistance, skin and mucous membranes	skin problems, anorexia, diarrhoea	
B3 (pantothene acid)	part of coenzyme A, Krebs-cycle	alopecia, anorexia, diarrhoea	
B6 (pyridoxine)	catalyst protein metabolism	skin problems, haematological problems	
biotine	catalyst fatty acid synthesis	coat and skin problems	
folic acid	catalyst AZ synthesis	haematological and skin problems	
B12 (cyanocobalamine)	catalyst cystine/ methiomine metabolism	anaemia, alopecia, growth problems	

Energy

All organic processes require energy for the body to function, produce tissue and to maintain body temperature for example. The energy required must be provided by food. In principal, dogs eat until their energy requirements have been met. However, due to causes such as boredom, the feeding regime and the tastiness of the food, there are many dogs that eat more than they need and become overweight. Due to this risk it is important to regularly check your dog's weight to ensure he is healthy.

A dog will store energy reserves as fat on the ribcage. On shorthaired dogs, you must be able to see the last two ribs, and on longhaired dogs you must be able to feel the ribs. Initially, feed your dog with the amount recommended on the food packaging and check your dog's condition once a week. You can adjust the amount you feed according to your dogs individual needs (what is right for one, may be too much for another based on their metabolic rate, and level of activity) Increase the amount of food if the ribs are becoming too pronounced, and decrease the amount if the ribs are disappearing under a layer of fat! Many puppies, particularly of breeds prone to skeletal growth problems, should be a little on the thinner side while growing.

Industrial food

Industrial dog foods can be divided into three categories depending on their moisture content: moist, semi-moist and dry food. Moist foods contain 70 - 85% water; the high moisture content makes it very tasty for dogs, but it spoils more easily, the quality is more difficult to maintain than with dry food, and it is relatively expensive.

Semi-moist food is dry enough that it does not have to be packed into cans, but there are no real advantages to this type of food. Dogs might initially prefer it to dry food, but it is still easily spoiled due to its higher moisture content.

Dry foods are the most economical and do not generally go off, which means that they keep for a comparatively long time. The specific manufacturing process makes it easier to ensure constant high quality levels. Technically speaking, mixers can also be termed as dry food, until they have had water added, at this point, they also spoil quite quickly. If you want to compare different types of food with each other, you will need to look at the dry matter (= product without water) contents and ingredients.

It is very difficult to judge the quality of dog food as the packaging does not provide all the information and may not contain any quality claims. It is therefore a matter of personal

choice, and you might want to request some further information from the manufacturer. Generally speaking, though, as with most things in life, you get what you pay for. That does not automatically mean that the most expensive food is the best food as you may be paying for advertising and such. The amount of faeces also gives an indication: the more faeces, the lower the food quality. This, however, does not apply to fibre-rich foods, such as diet foods, "light foods", senior foods and diabetic foods.

Food quality

There are a number of important points regarding the quality of dog food: the digestibility, the biological value (degree to which the nutrients can be absorbed into the tissue), the manufacturing process and the circumstances under which the food is kept until consumption.

Different terminology is used to indicate quality levels, the current product range includes super premium, premium, products for the medium segment and products for the economical segment. The lower the quality, the lower the price per kilogram. Top quality can only be delivered by manufacturers who have the best raw materials available, who conduct thorough research and who have a technologically advanced manufacturing process.

The first threat to the quality is oxidization of the ingredients. Light, oxygen and warmth are threats to food quality. Anti-oxidants are therefore essential in maintaining the quality of the ingredients; this coupled with hygienic handling of the food during preparation ensures a top quality product. Good-quality food is packaged in airtight packaging, which also keeps out the light, includes a best before date, batch code and manufacturing date.

Physiological phases

A good diet should take the physiological

phase of the individual dog into account. After all, the physiological phase largely determines what a dog needs in his diet. A growing dog produces a lot more tissue and therefore needs more building blocks than an adult dog. All these growth processes require a lot of energy, which means that the energy need is also higher, depending on the size of the dog, it will grow for 7 to 18 or even 24 months. During the growing period the puppy's digestive system is not fully developed and so can only cope with small volumes of food, it is important that the food is both energy dense (which allows for a smaller feeding volume) and balanced in nutrients for the age and stage in development. Puppies from a number of (usually) larger breeds have an increased risk of bone-related growth problems and must be fed a specifically adapted diet. It is also important to keep these puppies slim when they are growing, to prevent added stress on the skeleton.

Reproduction and lactation are very physically demanding on the bitch. When you consider that she has to produce both offspring and milk, it is logical that she will need to increase her energy levels. From the 6th week of the pregnancy, you will need to adjust

the amount you feed. Energy demands also increase if your dog is very active, if there is a lot of stress on muscle tissue, it will need energy to repair itself from time to time and there is also increasing 'wear' on the blood, which means that more nutrients are needed to produce plenty of blood cells. If you keep your dog in an outdoor kennel, it might also require more energy to stay warm and it might be more active due to being kept outdoors.
By examining the needs of dogs in different physiological phases, it is possible to develop a diet, which fulfils specific requirements according to the dog's circumstances. Obviously, this type of dog food requires scientific research and high-quality raw materials, which will be reflected in its price. Besides the physiological state of the dog, the size also affects the diet.
Research has shown that there are many differences between small and large dogs; both in terms of susceptibility to health problems and in anatomy and physiology. The manufacturers of the best dog foods take these differences into account. Different breeds, naturally, have their specific size requirements, and every breed also has its own characteristics, such as a special coat or even breed-specific health conditions. Breed-specific diets are therefore becoming increasingly popular. These foods are based on the special nutritional needs of the breed and some foods also contain substances, which help to prevent breed-specific health problems developing.

	Small dog	Difference*	Large dog
Growth period	8 months	3	24 months
Range of growth	20x birth weight	5	100x birth weight
Length canine tooth	4-5 mm	3	15-16 mm
Energy needs	132 Kcal/kg BW**	3	45 Kcal/kg BW**
Weight digestive tract	7% BW**	>2	2.8% BW**
Life expectancy	> 12 years	+/- 3	7 years

* Difference = factor ** BW = body weight

Over the last few years, increasing attention has been paid to the possible effect of dog food in addressing potential health risks. Certain substances are added to the food, for example to increase the burning of fat (L-carnitine), to prevent diarrhoea in puppies (zeolite), to support the cartilage (glucosamine and chondroitine sulphate), etc. The right food can make a significant contribution to the overall health of your dog.

Important guidelines

In general

Buy food only in an undamaged, sealed package and take advice from experts (vet, pet shop owner or breeder). Buying in bulk might be economical, but make sure that you have a sealed food bin to store it in. Put a week's supply in a bucket, and place the rest in a food bin in a dark, cool place. Always make sure that you use up or throw away the last bit and clean out the bin regularly!

Puppy food

Buy the most suitable food for your puppy, according to the advice of your vet or breeder. The basis for a healthy adult life is laid in the growth period and food plays an important role in this.

Adult dog

Choose the food which best suits your dog and adapt the amount you feed according to its condition. Ensure you reassess this regularly as varying factors such as age; metabolic rate and level of activity can play a role in the amount of food your dog requires.

Pregnant dog

The amount of food a bitch requires increases from the 6th week of pregnancy. In the past, bitches were often fed puppy food in the last stage of the pregnancy or during lactation.
However, with today's range of puppy foods, they might not all be suitable, so get expert advice on how best to feed your pregnant bitch.

Older dog

The dietary requirements of an older dog can change quite a lot. Scientifically speaking, older dogs need more easily digestible food, which stimulates the intestines, a normal protein content with high biological value and some support for the heart, the skeleton and to help boost its immune system.

Puppies, pregnant bitch and mother

Amount of food during pregnancy and suckling period

To ensure that the weight increase is no more than 20% on large bitches and no more than 30% on small bitches, it is important to keep a close eye on the weight of your pregnant bitch.

The more the weight increases, the higher the risk of problems during the birth. During pregnancy and suckling, the bitch must be fed a correctly composed diet to ensure that her food reserves are not completely exhausted. If she is fed inadequately during this highly demanding time, the bitch will have far more trouble recovering.

During pregnancy

A bitch is pregnant for approximately 63 days. Her food needs start to increase at around the 5th or 6th week of pregnancy. About 25% of the foetus develops during the first 6 weeks of the pregnancy; the remaining 75% of the foetus develops from weeks 6 to 9.

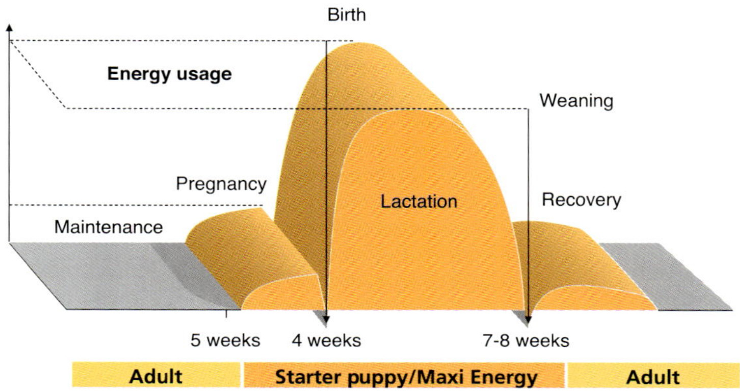

During the last trimester, your bitch will have a particularly high need for:
Energy: + 50 to 70%
Proteins: + 170 to 180%
Minerals: ++ (calcium, phosphorus)
Vitamins: ++

The increasing nutritional needs of the pregnant bitch are best met by feeding a specifically composed diet, from the fifth or sixth week onwards. Starter puppy foods or maxi energy foods are known to contain the required nutritional needs for this period. Besides needing more energy, the bitch also needs more proteins as well as a concentrated and easily digestible diet, as the uterus pushes onto the stomach during pregnancy, which decreases the stomach volume. This means the bitch cannot cope with large amounts of food per feeding at this time, so feed smaller amounts more often.

During suckling

The suckling period lasts for 4 to 5 weeks, and the puppies gradually suckle less from the 4th week onwards. While suckling her offspring, the bitch will have a much greater need for energy, as she must also produce the food for her litter. As mother's milk is very rich in energy and proteins, it is important that the bitch is fed a diet which is high in energy and proteins, and which is very easily digestible. The actual amount of food required varies hugely, and primarily depends on the size of the litter. The food needs of a suckling bitch may be as follows:

Energy: + 325%
Proteins: + 725%
Minerals: ++++ (calcium, phosphorus)
Vitamins: ++++

To prevent digestive problems, it is advisable to feed the bitch the same food from the last part of the pregnancy until the time that the puppies are fully weaned. The bitch's intestines are particularly sensitive to food changes during this important period. Within 24 hours, a puppy suckles more than twenty times from its mother. The bitch must produce 20 to 25% of a puppy's weight in milk to feed one puppy for one day (so multiply this by the number of puppies in the litter). The bitch may be fed ad lib during the suckling period, but do keep an eye on her condition.
Colostrum is the first milk that the bitch produces after the puppies are born. It is therefore very important that the puppies drink their mother's milk within the first 24 hours after birth. The colostrum contains anti-bodies against infections, which gives the puppies a good start to building up their own solid resistance. If the bitch produces too little milk, you will need to supplement it with special puppy milk.

Puppy during weaning
Immediately after birth the puppies depend entirely on their mother's milk as their only food source to stay alive. It is very important to check your puppies' growth during the

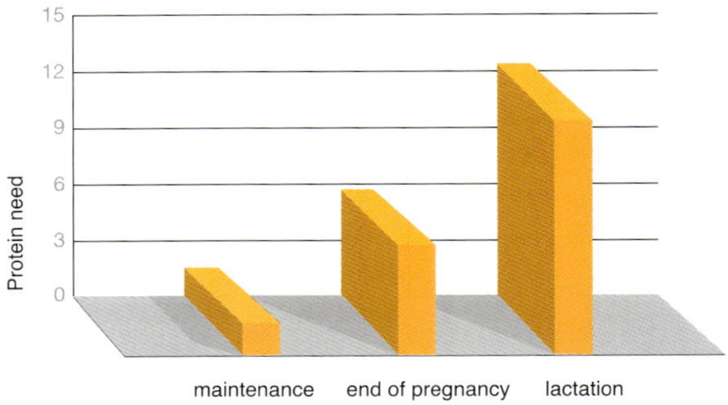

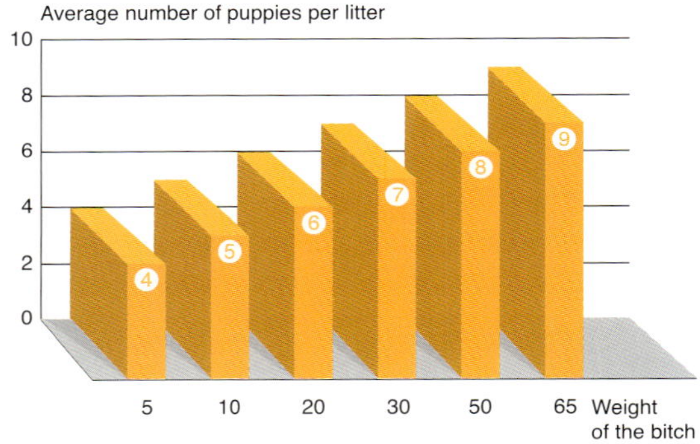

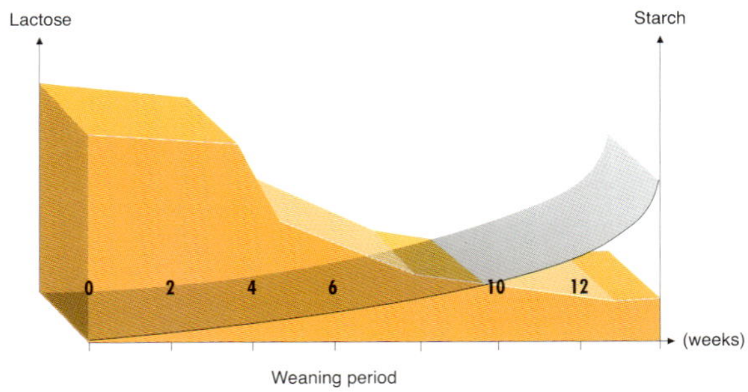

first few days by weighing them at exactly the same time every day. Weaning must be a smooth and gradual transition, so that the puppy and its digestion gets used to a completely new diet. When the puppy changes from a liquid diet to a solid diet, it is advisable to do this via an extra step.

Energy: + 50 to 70%
Proteins: + 170 to 180%
Minerals: ++ (calcium, phosphorus)
Vitamins: ++

Weaning - an important period

The first step in the weaning process begins after the third week, when you can start feeding the puppies small amounts of moistened food. During the weaning period, the puppies are quite prone to diarrhoea, which is at least partly due to their limited ability to digest starch. Compared to an adult dog, they only have a 5 - 10% ability to digest starch (see picture). To minimise the risk of diarrhoea and to ensure optimum digestion, feed the puppy a food that is easily digestible and has low starch content.

Ready-made foods

It is not easy for the average pet owner to put together a complete menu for a dog, which includes all the necessary proteins, fats, vitamins and minerals in just the right proportions and quantities. Meat alone is certainly not a complete meal for a dog as it contains too little calcium. A calcium deficiency over time will lead to bone defects, and for a fast-growing puppy, this can lead to serious skeletal deformities.

If you mix the food yourself, you can easily give your dog too much in terms of vitamins and minerals, which can also be bad for his health. These problems can be easily avoided by feeding a ready-made food of a good brand. These products are well balanced and contain everything your dog needs, in this instance, supplements such as vitamin preparations are superfluous. The amount of food your dog needs depends on its weight and activity level and you can find guidelines for this on the food packaging. Split the food into two meals per day if possible and always ensure there is a bowl of fresh drinking water next to the food bowl.

It is vital that you give your dog the time to digest his food properly; do not let him outside straight after a meal. A dog should also never play on a full stomach as this can cause bloat (gastric torsion), where the stomach becomes overstretched due to an excessive gas content. This can be fatal to your dog.

Because the nutritional needs of a dog depend, among other things, on its age and way of life, there are many different types of dog food available. There are light foods for less active dogs, energy foods for working dogs and senior foods for the older dog.

Dry puppy foods

There is a wide assortment of puppy chunks on the market. These chunks contain a higher content of growth-promoting nutrients, such as protein and calcium. There are special, puppy chunks available for various sizes of dogs, and it is important that you buy the dog food that matches the size of your dog. A Dobermann should be fed puppy food for a large sized dog, puppy chunks for smaller of medium sized dogs may promote too fast growth and can cause conditions such as hip and elbow-dysplasia (see chapter Health).

Canned foods, mixer and dry foods

Ready-made foods available at pet shops or in the supermarket can roughly be split into canned food, mixer and dry food. Whichever form you choose ensure that it is a complete food with all the necessary ingredients. The information is usually on the packaging.

Most dogs love canned food, and although the better brands are of good quality and composition, they do have one disadvantage: they are soft. A dog fed only on canned food will not benefit from the gently abrasive effects of dry food on its teeth, and may potentially develop problems such as plaque, and/or periodontitis. Alongside canned food, give your dog hard foods or a chew especially designed for his oral care and hygiene.

Mixer is a food consisting of chunks, dried vegetables and grains where almost all moisture has been extracted. The advantages of feeding a mixer are that it is light and keeps well in storage and you need only add a certain amount of water and the

meal is ready. It must never be fed without water, as without the extra fluid, the mixer will absorb the fluids present in the stomach, with serious results. Should your dog manage to get at the bag of mixer or dry chunks and devour its contents, give the dog very small amounts of water - half a cup - over extended (20 – 30 minutes) intervals.
Dry chunks have also had the moisture extracted but not to the same degree as the mixer.
The advantage of dry foods is that they are hard, forcing the dog to crunch, removing plaque and massaging the gums.

Dog chew products

Once in a while you will want to treat your Dobermann. However, avoid giving him bits of cheese or sausage as these contain too much salt and fat. There are various products available that a dog will find delicious and which are also healthy, especially for his teeth. You will find a large range of varying quality, and price in most pet shops.

The butcher's leftovers

The bones of slaughtered animals have traditionally been given to dogs and most dogs still consider them to be a great treat! But they are not without significant risks. Pork and poultry bones can splinter and cause serious injury to the intestines, so it is vital that you never give your dog this type of bone. However, beef bones are more suitable, as long as they have been cooked to kill off dangerous bacteria. Pet shops carry a range of smoked, cooked and dried abattoir leftover's, such as pigs' ears, tripe sticks and hoof chews.

Fresh meat

If you want to give your dog fresh meat occasionally always feed cooked (either boiled or roasted), never give it raw. Raw or partially cooked pork or chicken can contain life-threatening organisms. Chicken can be contaminated by the notorious salmonella bacteria, while pork can carry the incurable Aujeszky virus.

Buffalo or cowhide chews

Dog chews are mostly made of cowhide or buffalo hide. Chews are usually knotted or pressed hide and can come in the form of little shoes, twisted sticks, lollies, balls and various other shapes.

Munchy sticks

Munchy sticks are green, yellow, red or brown coloured sticks of various thicknesses. They consist of ground buffalo hide with a number of often, undefined, additives. Dogs usually love them because these sticks have been dipped in the blood of slaughtered animals, but the composition and quality of these treats is not always clear. Always choose a product with clearly described ingredients.

Something to drink

A dog can go days without eating if it must, but definitely not without drinking! Make sure your Dobermann always has a bowl of fresh water available. Food and water bowls of stainless steel are the easiest to keep clean and won't get chewed during the perils of puppyhood!

Overweight?

Today, obesity among dogs is an ever-increasing problem. A dog usually gains weight due to over-feeding and lack of exercise - medicines or disease are rarely the cause. Dogs that get too fat are often given too much food or too many treats between meals, and a dog often puts on weight following neutering or spaying. This is due to changes in hormone levels, making it less active, and less likely to burn energy. Finally, simply too little exercise and activity can lead to a dog becoming overweight.

To ascertain your dog is a healthy weight you should be able to feel its ribs, but not see them. If you cannot feel its ribs then your dog is too fat. Overweight dogs live a passive life; they play too little and tire quickly. They also suffer from all kinds of medical problems (problems with joints and the heart for example) as a consequence they usually die younger too.

So it is important to make sure your dog does not get too fat. Always follow the guidelines on food packaging, and adapt them if your dog is less active or gets lots of snacks. Try to make sure your dog gets plenty of exercise by playing and running with him as much as you can. If your dog starts to show signs of weight gain, you can switch to a low-calorie food. If he really is too fat and reducing his food quantity does not help, then a special diet is the only solution.

Care

Good daily care is extremely important for your Dobermann, as a well cared-for dog is less likely to become ill. Caring for your dog is not only necessary but also a pleasure. It is a wonderful chance for dog and owner to bond on a regular basis.

The coat

Caring for your Dobermann's coat involves regular brushing and combing, as well as checking for parasites such as fleas. How often a dog needs to be brushed and combed depends on the length of its coat.
Dobermanns are less demanding in this respect, as a shorthaired dog needs very little maintenance outside the moulting season. A healthy Dobermann has a shiny coat, which should be brushed once a week with a rubber massage brush. It is advisable to get a puppy used to being brushed from an early age by brushing it every day during its early puppyhood.

Brushing your dog every week should make bathing superfluous, and is not to be encouraged as the shampoo removes fat from the skin and coat. If, however, your dog has a good roll in something unpleasant, then wash it with a special dog shampoo, as the acidity level of your dog's skin is different to that of human skin, so it may well react to your own shampoo. A vet can prescribe special medicinal shampoos for some skin problems. Always follow the instructions to the letter.

During the moulting period (twice a year), you should give your Dobermann's coat a stiff brushing every day. This is essential as brushing promotes the growth of the new coat

and prevents your furniture being buried under dog hairs. Brush in both the direction the coat is growing and in the opposite direction until no more loose hairs come out of the coat.
It is important you use the right equipment for taking care of the coat. Combs should not be too sharp and you should use a rubber or natural hairbrush.

Good flea prevention is highly important to avoid skin and coat problems. Fleas must be treated not only on the dog itself but also in its surroundings (see the chapter on Parasites). Coat problems can also occur due to an allergy to certain food substances, in such cases, a vet can prescribe a hypoallergenic diet.

Teeth

Dobermanns generally experience few dental problems, although they may suffer from tartar and bad breath in old age. To prevent this, you should have the teeth checked for tartar when taking your dog to the veterinarian for its annual vaccinations, as bad breath can be the result of dental problems.
Bad breath can also be caused by stomach problems or certain foods. If this is the case it is advisable to switch to a different diet.

It is important that you check your dog's teeth regularly as it needs healthy teeth in order to eat properly and stay in good condition. If you suspect your dog is suffering from a dental problem consult your vet. Regular feeds of hard dry food can also help keep your dog's teeth clean and healthy and there are special dog chews on the market that help prevent plaque and help keep your dog's breath fresh – but brushing your dog's teeth regularly is the best way of maintaining good dental health. You can use special toothbrushes for dogs, but a finger wrapped in a small piece of gauze will also do the job. Brush your dog's

Schematic representation of the teeth

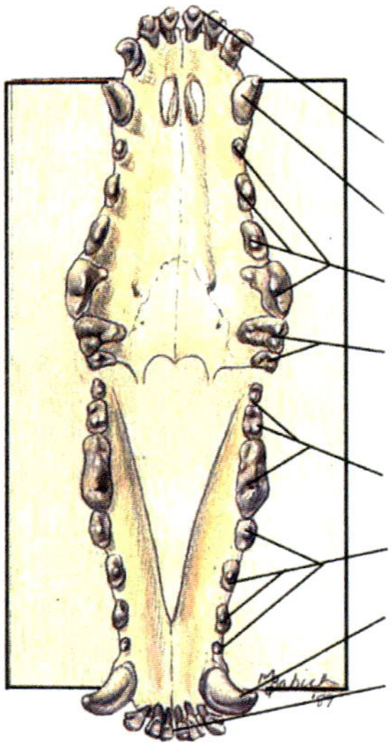

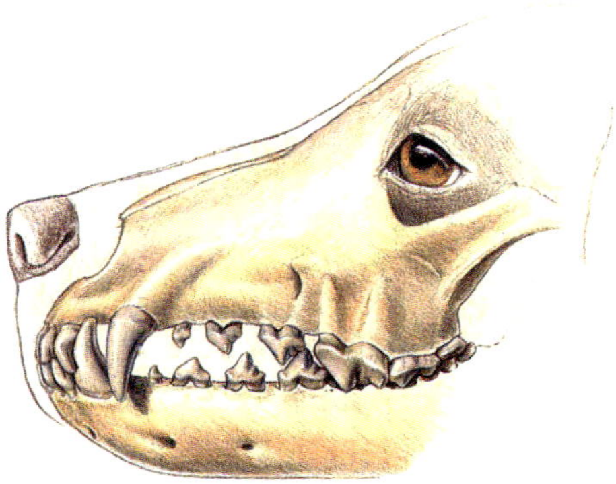

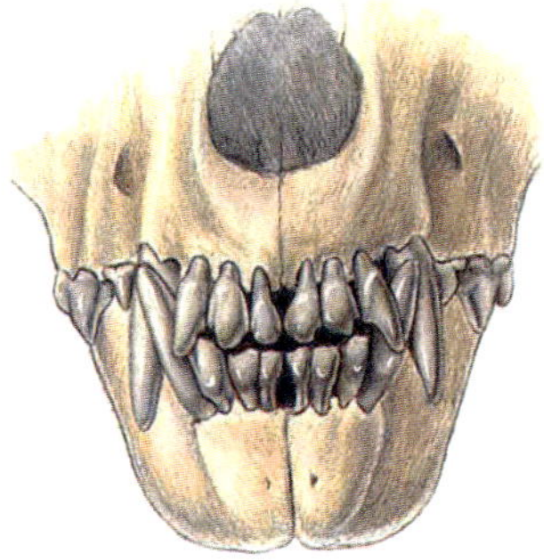

Left: profile of the teeth
Right: front view of the teeth

teeth throughout his puppyhood and he will soon grow used to it.
You can even teach an older dog to have his teeth cleaned, use a dog chew as a reward and he will quickly learn to accept it.

Eyes

A dog's eyes should be cleaned regularly as discharge can build up in the corners of the eye - you can easily remove it by wiping it downwards with your thumb or a piece of tissue or toilet paper.

Keeping your dog's eyes clean takes a matter of moments, but is an important daily task. Yellow discharge could be a sign of infection, in which case eye drops prescribed by the vet should quickly clear up the problem.

Ears

It is important that you check your Dobermann's ears at least once a week. Their ear channels can sometimes be very narrow and can quickly become blocked and contaminated. If your dog's ears are very dirty or blocked with wax it is essential that you clean them. This should preferably be done with a clean cotton cloth (not cotton wool), moistened with lukewarm water or baby oil, or alternatively you can buy an ear cleaner from your vet. NEVER penetrate the ear canal with an object. If you neglect your dog's ears there is a significant risk of infection. A dog that is constantly scratching at its ears, or shaking its head may well be suffering from dirty ears, an ear infection or ear mites, in which case it is essential you contact your vet immediately.

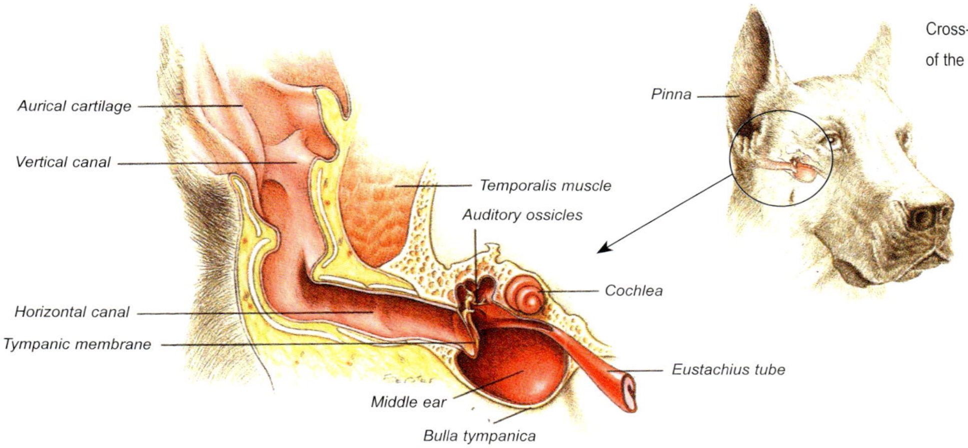

Cross-sectional view of the ear

Nails

Nails usually wear down naturally if the dog regularly walks on hard surfaces, in which case there is no need to clip them. Nevertheless it is worth checking their length now and again, especially if your Dobermann doesn't often walk on roads. Using a piece of paper, you can easily see whether its nails are too long - if you can push the paper between the nail and the ground when the dog is standing, then the nail is the right length.

Nails that are too long can become a problem as the dog can injure itself when scratching. You can buy special nail clippers in pet shops, but be careful not to clip back too far as you can cut into the quick, which can bleed profusely.
If you feel unsure about carrying out this important task, ask a vet or a groom to do it for you.
Special attention is needed for the dewclaw, the nail on the inside of the hind leg, which needs clipping at regular intervals to ensure it does not cause an injury.

Rearing

In order to enjoy dog ownership to the full it is important that you train your dog to be obedient. This does not have to be dull for you or your puppy, and if approached with the right attitude training can be fun and rewarding for both of you.
Praise and consistency are essential when training a dog. Rewarding your puppy for good behaviour with your voice, a pat or something tasty will soon teach it to be obedient. A puppy-training course can also be helpful.

When dealing with your dog, it is also useful to know something about the life and behaviour of dogs, and their ancestors (wolves, in the wild).

In the wild, wolves live in packs. Our domestic dogs view their human family as their pack. Every pack has a hierarchy, this means that there is one boss - the alpha animal - and all the other animals are ranked according to importance, right to the lowest position, the omega animal. There is a constant battle for the alpha spot in the pack. When you take a dog into your home, it is very important to make it clear where its place is in the family. This is simply done by following twelve rules. In this chapter, we deal with the 'rules of the pack', what they are, how you can apply them and what you can do and what you should not do.

The rules of the pack

Rule 1

The Alpha dog chooses a place to sleep, and no one challenges him.

The alpha dog chooses its own place to sleep and this is always respected by the animals lower in the hierarchy. If an animal lower in the hierarchy comes close to the resting alpha, the latter will growl to make it clear that the inferior dog must not approach. If the inferior animal approaches anyway, there is a real risk that the alpha will bite. This rule not only applies to resting and sleeping, it also includes access to places, which are prohibited to the inferior animal.

The alpha rules apply to any situation in which an animal high in the hierarchy asserts his authority over an inferior animal – it does not necessarily have to be the 'official' pack leader.

Advice

- Never let your dog sleep on your bed.
- The bedroom should ideally be forbidden territory for your dog.
- You can also prohibit access to other parts of the house. This makes it clear to the dog that you are higher in the hierarchy.
- Never try to take away your dog's safe place.
- Never let your dog take away your place.
- Never let your dog refuse people access to certain places.

Rule 2

The alpha male has the highest position.

In a pack of dogs, you often see the pack leader lying in a higher place than the rest of the pack, in order to assert his authority as the alpha dog.

Domestic dogs wishing to establish their dominance over you may attempt to lie in a high position – this behaviour must be stopped immediately to prevent your dog taking the alpha role in the pack. Dogs, which are lower down in the hierarchy, would never dare to demonstrate such behaviour.

Advice

- When you notice that your dog wants to lie on a higher position while you are present, do not allow it.
- If, for example you are sitting on the stairs and your dog comes to sit with you, make sure that it does not sit on a higher step than you.
- Never let your dog crawl on to your lap without your permission.

Rule 3

The alpha male eats first.

When the pack has caught a large prey, it is not necessarily divided up democratically. The alpha dog always eats first, possibly sharing with the alpha bitch. The rest of the pack must wait until the leader has finished.

The alpha male will decide when the rest of the pack gets its food. He may well decide that the others do not get anything at all, in which case he simply hides remains of the prey and moves away. This can be seen as a challenge by the alpha to the inferior dogs. If an inferior animal dares to approach the food, the alpha will growl loudly and bite the challenger in the neck to correct it, or take the food away from it to display his higher position.

Advice

- Prepare your dog's food and place it out of reach, then go and have your dinner before feeding the dog.
  Only feed your dog when the whole family has finished. Place the food on the floor and give the 'stay' command before allowing your dog to approach his food.
- Place a toy on the floor close to your dog, and as he approaches remove the toy. Repeat this a few times and eventually the dog will soon stop trying to take the toy - this is the moment when your dog acknowledges your superiority.
- Never feed your dog anything while the family is having dinner as this gives the dog the same position in the hierarchy as you.

- Be careful with food envy! Never take food away from your dog and stay away from its food bowl when it is eating.

Food envy

Many dogs refuse to give up things they carry in their mouth (food, toys). If you do try to take these things from your dog, he is likely to growl. We can often see the same behaviour in dogs that are eating, this behaviour is called 'food envy' – and this is not acceptable behaviour. This can be prevented by training a puppy at young age that he should give up anything to his master that is asked of him. Training this with a toy that your puppy has to give up when asked, will prove to work well.

Rule 4

Playing, not fighting, is the way to establish hierarchy.

A dog can determine and confirm hierarchical positions during play. For young dogs, in particular, playing is also a way to learn to live in a group, and to slowly determine their status within the pack, as pet dogs often remain playful well into their old age.

If dogs constantly fought over their positions in the pack hierarchy, there would be a lot of casualties - in the wild an injured animal is extremely vulnerable and weakens the pack as a whole. Therefore dogs use play as a means of establishing the hierarchy. When two strange dogs meet they can respond to each other aggressively, as they are not members of the same pack, this has nothing to do with establishing a hierarchy, but with protecting their territory.

Territory

The territory is the domain of the pack. This territory may be several kilometres across and is divided into three different sectors. The outer circle of the territory is the first line of defence and pack members will make it clear to intruders that they are not welcome. If an intruder does manage to get through, into the middle circle, the pack will attack him. However, he will be given the chance to escape during this attack. The innermost circle is the centre of the pack; this is where puppies are reared and where the whole pack retreats to rest. Defending this area is a matter of life and death.
In the Western World humans live in very close proximity so it is not surprising that dogs have so many territorial conflicts. A dog will only view his garden as the centre of his territory; the rest is outside your garden fence. This means that the territories of dogs living close together overlap each other. Even when walking a dog on the lead a dog still has a territory. It is a mobile territory, and the dog sees itself as the centre, that needs to be defended.

It is therefore not surprising that two dogs often react aggressively to each other when taken out for a walk. After all, the centre of the territory must be defended.

Advice

- Always keep games under your control: make sure you determine the course of a game, not your dog.
- It is important to be aware that dogs use play as a means of establishing hierarchy – so make sure you always 'win' the game.
  If you think that your dog is trying to dominate the game, stop immediately and ignore him completely for a while.

Don'ts

- Never let your dog dominate the game.
- Never let your dog determine how or what you are going to play - that is your decision.

Rule 5

The alpha wins every game.

When dogs are playing, you can see that a superior animal will always assume a higher position than an inferior animal. The superior animal will decide when the game is over and it will always win.

Advice

- Make sure that you always win the last game when playing with your dog. It is possible to let your dog win a game once in a while, but you must dominate the major part of it. How many games your dog is allowed to win depends on the hierarchical relationship between you and your dog. A dominant dog should never be allowed to win. A submissive dog can be allowed to feel like a winner once in a while.
- Never let your dog win the last game.
- Never finish a retrieve game by throwing the object, as if the dog ends up with the toy in his possession in his mind he will have 'won'. Equally, it is essential when playing a tug-of-war game that you finish the game in possession of the toy. It is particularly important in a tug-of-war game that you always start and end the game.

Rule 6

The alpha always has right of way.

If a superior animal moves through the pack, all the inferior animals will move out of its way.

Advice

- If your dog is coming towards you and wants to move past you, do not move aside - let him find a path around you.

- Always ensure your dog moves out of your path when required. Never step over a dog, even when it is asleep.

Rule 7

The highest in the hierarchy will always go through a narrow passageway first.

A narrow passageway is a very broad term in the domestic context. It is not only a doorway or a gate, but also the alleyway between two houses, the space between parked cars or even a forest path.

In a pack, when dogs are let out of their kennels, it is always the animal highest in the hierarchy, which exits first. Dogs often run ahead when out on a walk.

Advice

- Open a door a little. If your dog wants to go through, close it – however, be very careful that your dog's nose does not get caught! Repeat this until your dog no longer attempts to go through the door, then exit first and allow your dog to follow.
- Sometimes your dog will try to go ahead of you through a passageway, which cannot be closed with a door or gate. In this case, keep your dog on a four to five metre long lead and walk towards the passageway. If your dog tries to go ahead, turn around and walk away from the entrance – the dog will feel a pull from the lead as it tightens and will quickly learn to follow you. Repeat these steps until your dog no longer attempts to go through the passageway first.
- You must never try to physically prevent a dog from going through a passageway first. If you try to discipline your dog in such a manner, it will soon learn that it simply has to be faster than you.
- Never let your dog pull on the lead.

Rule 8

All pack members pay respect to the alpha male every day.

All dogs in a pack confirm their submissive position every day by following the rules of the established hierarchy on a daily basis. They devote most of their time to the alpha dog, which they honour by greeting first for example. Everything that occurs within a pack reflects the hierarchy.

Advice

- Observe the rules of the pack on a daily basis.
- Always respect the hierarchy.
- Always show respect for those superior (for children, this is the parents).
- When eating, when wiping your feet after a walk or when going through a passageway, make sure that you always come first and that your dog always comes last.

- Always greet the highest members of the hierarchy first, this means that a dog must be greeted last according to its status within the pack.
- According to the rules of the pack, a superior animal must never let an inferior animal have an advantage - and this must be observed at all times. Never greet your dog before its superiors, as this will confuse its position within the hierarchy.

Rule 9

The alpha dog knows best.

The pack leader decides everything that goes on within a pack. He decides when to sleep, when to hunt, when to play, when to eat, etc. No other dog within the pack will make decisions that contradict those of the leader.

Advice

- As the boss, it is essential that you make all the decisions for your dog within the human/dog pack. You decide when your dog is allowed to go for a walk, to eat, play and sleep etc.
- Never let your dog decide. If he tries to persuade you to feed, play or take him for a walk, ignore him until you choose to initiate an activity.

Rule 10

An inferior member of the pack pays attention to the alpha.

The alpha never approaches an inferior animal, unless it wants to reprimand it.
An inferior animal always approaches a superior animal, and assumes a submissive posture (head low, ears back, tail low).

Active submission

Inferior dogs sometimes approach the alpha. In this case, they assume a low posture; the ears are pinned back, the tail is carried low and the body is generally held low and parallel to the ground. When an inferior animal reaches the superior, it will lick the corners of its mouth. This is a social gesture which dogs inherited from their ancestors, confirming its submissive position. We call this active submission - the inferior dog initiates the submission.

Passive submission

In passive submission, the inferior animal also assumes a low posture. However, in this instance the superior animal initiates the submission. The alpha approaches the inferior animal with a superior posture, and the inferior dog will react immediately and assume a submissive posture. If it does not do this, it will be reprimanded by the superior animal.

Advice

- Always make your dog approach you.
- Regularly play games of chase where your dog must follow you.
- Only ever approach your dog when you need to reprimand it.
- Never approach your dog, particularly when he is lying in his safe place. By initiating contact you are assuming an inferior position and are consequently undermining your position as the pack leader.

Rule 11

The alpha alone has the right to ignore other members of the pack.

The alpha will often ignore its inferiors as they pass by whereas the inferior would never dare to ignore its superior! In general, a pack leader will usually ignore the lowest members of the pack – and the job of caring for the youngest and most insignificant dogs usually falls to the rest of the group.

Every member of the pack must pay attention to the alpha. This ensures the group stays together - where the leader goes, the rest follow.

Advice

- Regularly ignore your dog when passing by, this confirms your position in the pack as his superior.
- It is advisable to ignore your dog if he starts to demand your attention too frequently. Try to avoid punishing your dog through negative reinforcement - to a dog any attention is better than no attention at all.

- Never let your dog ignore you, use plenty of positive reinforcement to maintain his interest in you.

Rule 12

A superior animal awards privileges to the rest of the pack.
Superior members of the pack will award privileges to those below it according to the inferior animals behaviour. Those at the bottom of the hierarchy are given the least privileges to maintain the pecking order. Equally, if an animal begins to misbehave its privileges can be withdrawn.

Advice

- Once you have established the hierarchy within your human/dog pack you can begin to award your dog some privileges by relaxing some of the pack rules. This will allow your dog to move a little closer to the rest of the family in terms of hierarchy, so it is important you still maintain some distance as the alpha member of the pack - the dog is not your equal!

Don'ts

- Never allow a dog privileges that are equal to other members of the pack as he will soon take advantage and attempt to challenge the established hierarchy.

Disobedience

A disobedient dog is unpleasant for all concerned, and can make dog ownership a total misery! To avoid this it is vital you start your dog's training from the first day you bring him home.

If you do not give your dog strict ground rules, and put an immediate stop to undesirable behaviour bad habits can quickly form. In the case of dog training, prevention is definitely better than cure! It is generally a good idea to attend an expert training class with your dog alongside regular training sessions at home.

Always be consistent when training, reward good behaviour and correct annoying habits. Use positive, rather than negative reinforcement to establish a strong bond between you and your dog. This means ignoring anything negative and showering your dog with praise when he gets something right. For example, if your dog is slow to recall, do not punish him for making you wait when he eventually comes, as he will quickly associate you with negativity. Instead reward him for approaching you and he will quickly link you with positive experiences.

House-training

House training is one of the first, and most important lessons any puppy must learn. The basis for good house-training is total vigilance!

Always put a puppy out at the same times throughout the day; in the morning as soon as he is awake, before and after meals, every time he has been asleep or has been playing, and in the evenings before bedtime. Follow these rules and he will quickly learn where and when he is allowed to do his business. Praise him profusely each time he gets it right and allow him to play a little outside after he has relieved himself. If he does have the occasional accident in the house, take him outside immediately - do not punish him as he is learning, and the responsibility for this early training really lies with you.

Of course, it is not always possible to go out after every snack or snooze. Lay newspapers at different spots in the house. Whenever the pup needs to do its business,

place it on a newspaper. After some time it will start to look for a place itself. Then start to reduce the number of newspapers until there is just one left, at the front or back door. The puppy will learn to go to the door if it needs to relieve itself. Then you put it on the lead and go out with it. Finally you can remove the last newspaper. Your puppy is now house-trained.

First exercises

To get the right result it is important to be clear and consistent during training. Commands should be short and clear, such as 'Lie down!' or 'Stay there!' Use a clear tone and ensure that each command is different so your puppy can distinguish each one.
It is important to be consistent once you have chosen the commands you are going to use. If you want the dog to lie down, it is no use using 'Lie down!' once and 'Lay!' the next time, as this will prove to be very confusing. Once the dog has understood the intention, it should only be necessary to call a command once, clearly and in an appropriate tone. If he does not react immediately, make a disapproving sound while walking towards him. Try to avoid shouting as this rarely has the desired effect. Dogs have exceptional hearing, and commands should be given in a quiet and preferably soft tone. Keep raising your voice for exceptional situations, and the shock factor will prove to be very effective!

The first lesson for any Dobermann is to learn his name. Use it as much as possible from the first day onwards, followed by a friendly 'here'. Reward him with your voice and encourage him to come all the way up for a pat and a cuddle. Your puppy will quickly recognise the intention and has now learned its first command in a playful manner. Do not punish your young puppy as he is learning and will not be wilfully misbehaving. Once he has learnt this first important lesson you can move on gradually to basic commands such as 'Sit'. 'Down' and 'Stay'.

You can teach a Dobermann to sit by holding a tasty treat above his nose and slowly moving it back over his head. The puppy's head will also move backwards until its hind legs slowly go down, you can place an encouraging hand on his hindquarters too - at that moment say 'Sit! Once he is sitting reward him immediately with the treat. After a few attempts, he will quickly begin to make the connection between the command, the action, and the reward. Use the 'Sit!' command before you give your dog his food, put him on the lead or before he is allowed to cross the street.

You can teach your puppy the 'Down' command in a similar fashion. In this instance lure the dog down by moving the treat until your hand reaches the ground. The dog will also move its forepaws forwards and down, and you can help once again by placing your hand on his back and gently pressing. Use the command 'down' alongside this action and reward him as soon as his body reaches the floor.
You will need the help of another person to teach the command 'Come!'. One person holds the dog while the other stands at a distance of about fifteen metres before enthusiastically calling 'Come!' At this point the dog is released and should run towards the person calling him, where he should be showered with praise.

The stay command can be taught by first putting the dog into a 'Sit' or a 'Down' - then use the command 'Stay!' while showing him the palm of your hand before stepping back one pace. If the dog moves with you, quietly put it back in position, and repeat the command. Do not react angrily if he follows you as this is a learning curve and he will soon catch on. Once your Dobermann stays reward him abundantly. Do not let leave him in a stay for more than a few seconds in the beginning.
Once your puppy understands what is expected, you can gradually increase the time and distance of the stay.

Courses
It is strongly advisable to attend a training course with your Dobermann to ensure he is given every chance to grow up in to your ideal dog. Fun and informative training courses are available across

the country and are a great way for you to bond with your dog.
It is best to begin with a puppy course that is specially designed to provide the basic training and socialisation a dog needs to be a well-behaved citizen.
The class will also cover obedience and will help you teach your Dobermann basic commands.
The next step after this is a course for young dogs. This course repeats the basic exercises learned during puppyhood and ensures that the growing dog does not get into bad habits. After this, the dog can move on to more complex obedience course for adult dogs. For more information on where to find suitable courses in your area, contact the Kennel Club.

Play and toys

There are lots of fun games you can play with your dog, such as retrieving, tug-of-war, hide-and-seek and catch. Dobermanns adore all these games. A tennis ball is ideal for retrieving; and you can play tug-of-war with an old sock or a special tugging rope. Play tug-of-war only when your dog is at least one year old, as a puppy must first get its second teeth and then they need several months to strengthen.
You can use almost anything for a game of hide-and-seek, and a frisbee is ideal for catching games. Never use a very small ball when playing with your dog as it can easily get lodged in his throat.

Play is extremely important, as not only does it strengthen the bond between you and your dog but it also provides you both with plenty of exercise. Always make sure that you

are in control of all play and start and end every game. Only finish the game when the dog has brought back the ball or frisbee, and make sure you always win the tug-of-war, as this will confirm your dominant position in the hierarchy. When you are not playing, keep the toys out of reach of the dog so he does not forget their significance. When choosing a special dog toy, remember that dogs can be quite destructive, even with toys they love - so always buy toys of good quality that cannot easily be destroyed.

Avoid playing with sticks and twigs with your dog as they can easily splinter, causing pieces of wood to stick in your dog's throat or intestines – potentially causing serious health problems. Equally, throwing sticks or twigs can be dangerous as they can get stuck in your dog's mouth, which again can be a serious health risk.

If you want to be little more ambitious with your Dobermann's training there are several dog sports that can be attempted - such as Competitive Obedience and Agility.

Aggression

A properly socialised and rigorously brought-up Dobermann is practically never aggressive, but even they can sometimes be difficult with other animals or people. It's therefore a good idea to understand a little about the background of aggression in dogs.

In general there are two different types of aggressive behaviour; the anxious aggressive dog and the dominant aggressive dog.
An anxious aggressive dog will pull its ears back, show his teeth and adopt a position low to the ground. When a dog behaves in this way it is generally because he is very frightened and feels cornered. As he is unable to run away, an anxious aggressive dog will bite his victim anywhere he can in an attempt to defend himself as he feels under threat. The attack is usually brief and as soon as the dog can see a way to escape, he flees. In a confrontation with other dogs, the anxious aggressive dog will usually lose. However, if the people or dogs involved in the confrontation display fear he can become even more aggressive. If your dog starts to behave in this way it is essential you seek professional advice as the situation can easily escalate and become dangerous.

The dominant aggressive dog's body language is very different; his ears stand up and his tail is raised and stiff. The dominant aggressive dog is extremely self-assured and will hold a superior position within the hierarchy of his pack. The attack is a display of power rather than a consequence of fear. This dog needs to know who is the boss. It must be brought up rigorously and with a strong and consistent hand. An obedience course can help. Also you can seek professional help in dealing with this serious problem.

A dog may also bite when it is in pain as a natural defensive reaction. In this case try to reassure the dog as much as possible and reward him for letting you get to the painful spot. Be careful, because a dog in pain may also bite its owner. Muzzling can help in this situation. Never punish a dog for this type of aggression!

Fear

The source of anxious behaviour can often be traced to the first months of a dog's life – especially if there has been a lack of socialisation during this time. Puppyhood has a huge impact on behaviour in adult life and a dog that has never encountered humans,

other dogs or animals during this period will be instinctively afraid of them later. This fear is common with Dobermanns brought up in a barn or kennel, with almost no contact with humans. As mentioned above, fear can lead to aggressive behaviour, so it is important that a puppy gets as many new experiences as possible in the first months of his life. Take your puppy with you into town in the car or on the bus, walk with it down busy streets and allow it to have plenty of contact with humans, other dogs and other animals.

It is very difficult to turn an anxious, poorly socialised dog into a real pet – and you must be prepared to devote a huge amount of time and energy to the task. Ensure that you reward him often and give the dog plenty of time to adapt and, over time, he will learn to trust you and become less anxious. Try not to force an anxious dog into new experiences, instead use gentle coaxing techniques. An obedience class can also prove extremely helpful here.
An anxious, unsocialised dog can be especially afraid of strangers. Give visitors to your house a tasty treat to greet the dog with and he will soon start to associate new people with positive experiences.

Dogs are often frightened of things like thunderstorms and fireworks. In these cases try to ignore the anxious behaviour.
If you react to a dog's whimpering and whining, he will begin to see it as a means of attracting your attention, whereas if you ignore his fear completely, the dog will quickly learn that nothing is wrong. You can speed up this 'learning process' by rewarding positive behaviour.

Rewarding

Rewarding forms the foundations of good dog training. Rewarding good behaviour is far more effective than punishing bad behaviour – and is also a lot more fun! Over time dog training methods dogs have gradually changed. In the past the way to correct bad behaviour was often a sharp pull on the lead, whereas today, experts view rewarding as a positive means of reinforcing good behaviour. There are many ways to reward a dog; you can give him pat or a friendly word, or offer a tasty treat. Food is often the quickest way to teach a puppy, so make sure you always have something delicious in your pocket to reward good behaviour. Another form of reward is play. Reward a positive training session with a game with a special toy kept only for these occasions. As soon as you have finished playing, put the toy away, and your dog will soon start to associate it with good behaviour and positive experiences. Rewarding good behaviour is a fantastic training tool, but occasionally you may need to correct habitual bad behaviour. In this instance a firm 'no', followed by totally ignoring the dog should suffice. Again, consistency in all your actions is key in good upbringing of your Dobermann.

Barking

Dogs that bark too much and too often are a nightmare for anyone within earshot! A dog-owner may tolerate barking up to a point, but neighbours are often annoyed by the unnecessary noise. Do not encourage your puppy to bark and yelp; and correct such behaviour with a firm 'quiet'.

A dog will sometimes bark for long periods when left alone as he may feel abandoned or afraid and is trying to get someone's attention. There are special training programmes for this problem, where dogs learn that being alone is nothing to be afraid of, and that their owner will always return.

You can gradually train your dog to become accustomed to being left alone. Leave the room and come back in at once, reward your dog if he stays quiet. Gradually increase the length of your absences and keep rewarding as long as he remains calm and quiet. Never punish the dog after he has been barking as by then it is too late and he will not understand what he has done wrong - which could make the problem worse. Never go back into the room while the dog is barking, as he will view this as a reward. Leaving the radio switched on for company during your absence can sometimes help make the dog feel more relaxed. Eventually he will learn that you always return and will not feel the need to bark when left alone. If the problem does not seem to be resolving itself naturally consult a dog behaviourist or training expert.

Never leave your dog alone for more than a few hours.

Destructiveness

Destructiveness is often the result of boredom. A bored dog will look for something to distract himself with, so always make sure your dog has enough toys and chews to keep him occupied. Do not give him too many toys at once, but instead provide a variety - which you can constantly swap around - keeping your dog entertained.

At four or five months your puppy will start teething. This often causes pain and irritation, which the dog will attempt to combat through chewing on things. Ensure that during this phase you provide your puppy with chews and try and keep him away from the furniture! Take care to take away the last small pieces of the chews, because a dog can quickly choke on it. A puppy will often take it in its mouth in one piece and it can then wind up stuck in its throat.

Chasing

Some dogs have the annoying habit of chasing other animals, joggers or cyclists. If your puppy starts to show an inclination to chase it is vital you immediately deal with this behaviour before it becomes a bad habit. The best way to do this is to do attention exercises with your dog.
Make sure that you are the most interesting and exciting thing in your puppy's world and try to keep his attention while tempting distractions pass you by. If your puppy stays focused on you - reward him lavishly!

Walking on the lead

It is important that your Dobermann walks properly on the lead. Walking a powerful Dobermann that pulls on his lead, or walks irregularly, can be very tiring! Learning to follow off the lead is too difficult for a puppy, so start with a few walks on the lead. It is recommended that your dog follows on your left-hand side. This is the usual side used in training courses that you might want to take part in with your dog later. Of course, you can also use the right-hand side, as long as you stay consistent. Otherwise your dog may get confused, and forming habits is very important for a dog. Start teaching your dog to walk on the lead by putting on a soft leather (not too narrow) collar and leave it on for a few days. At the beginning, the puppy will probably try to pull this off, but over time he will get used to it automatically. Try to start practising during the day in a quiet place. Make it a habit for your puppy to do his business first, and let him free for a while so that he can play. Then he will have let off some steam and will be better able to concentrate on his training. Always try to get your dog to sit quietly beside you before letting him loose, but do not force this. After all, learning everything at once is a tall order. Hold your puppy by the collar, release the lead, wait a moment and then call his name followed by the command "Run!" in an inviting way. Then run a few steps with him

before letting him free. Your puppy must now be allowed to go his own way for the time you have allowed. Let him investigate everything, run and dig to his heart's content. Doing things on his own initiative can only help your dog's development.

After playing, it's time for your puppy to 'go to work'. At first he does not think much of having to walk with you. As soon as he feels the resistance of the lead on his collar, he will lie down, sit or try anything he can to get out of the collar. Get down on your haunches, call your puppy by his name in a friendly manner and carefully pull the lead towards you. Your puppy will soon give up his protest, and has now established the link that walking with his master is something pleasurable.

Dogs usually run happily to the door as soon as their master picks up their lead, but sometimes, perhaps, your puppy might not feel like going out. If he refuses to walk with you, give him a gentle tug on the lead. Never drag him because this can be bad for his joints and he will only find walking on the lead unpleasant. This will act against you if you want your dog to walk properly later.

Once your Dobermann puppy has mastered walking on the lead, and understands there is no point in refusing to go, then he will try another trick. He will start to pull at the lead. You can correct this too with short tugs on the lead and the command 'heel!' or 'better!' Whatever commands you choose is completely up to you, but keep them short and never change them again. Make sure different commands do not sound alike; a dog responds to a sound, and not to what you say.

Once walking goes well in quiet streets, look for a busier area. Keep the exercises short for the time being. Five intensive minutes with your puppy are enough. Stay calm and praise him. Your voice is a great support in any situation. Now it is time to cross the 't's and dot the 'i's. Shorten the lead until your Dobermann's head is parallel with your knees. If he stays back or pulls forward too much, give him a little tug on the lead with the command 'heel!' or 'better!'. When this is going well, you loosen the lead again, but keep correcting as soon as your puppy makes a mistake.

With the necessary patience and perseverance, you will have your dog walking properly beside you on the lead at six months. You should not expect any more than that. Many dogs are entered for certain courses because their master wants a result too fast. Wait a month or so longer before training a certain aspect rather than getting half the result too fast. Trying to force the dog will also only achieve the opposite to what you want. The dog will notice that you are not relaxed. This will only cause negative emotions, whereby you will only get a result with difficulty, if at all.

Breeding

Dogs follow their instincts, and consequently breeding is a fairly straightforward process. Most pet owners choose not to breed from their dogs, but it is still worth knowing a little about it to help you understand why dogs behave the way they do.

Liability

If you are planning to breed from your Dobermann it is important to be aware that a breeder is responsible for the quality of the puppies he breeds.

The Kennel Club places strict conditions on dogs used for breeding (see the chapter "Health"). If you want to breed a litter for fun, but do not have the relevant experience, you can ask the breed association for advice. Be extremely careful, because if the puppies you breed show any hereditary abnormalities in later life, you may be held liable by the new owners for any costs arising from inherited defects. The veterinary costs can be enormous, as well as the obvious implications of breeding dogs with significant health problems.

The female in season

It is a myth that it is better for a bitch's health to produce a litter. In reality, most spayed bitches lead long healthy lives, which are often improved by not having puppies! Bitches become sexually mature at about eight to twelve months, at which point they have their first season – which lasts for two or three weeks. During the first ten days they discharge little drops of blood and they become steadily more attractive to males. The bitch is fertile during the second half of her season, and will accept a male to mate. So the best time for mating is between the tenth and thirteenth day of her season. A bitch's first season is often shorter and lighter than those that follow. If you do want to breed from your bitch, you must wait until after her first and the second season. Most bitches go into season twice per year.

If you plan to breed with your Dobermann in the future, then spaying is obviously not an option.

Phantom pregnancy

A phantom pregnancy is actually not that uncommon. The female behaves as if she has a litter and takes all kinds of things to her basket and treats them like puppies. Her teats swell up and sometimes milk is actually produced. The female will sometimes behave aggressively towards humans or other animals, as if she is defending her young. Phantom pregnancies usually begin two months after a season and can last a number of weeks.

If it happens to a bitch once, it will often then occur after every season.
If this is a problem, spaying is the best solution, because continual phantom pregnancies increase the risk of womb or teat conditions. In the short term a hormone treatment is worth trying, also perhaps giving the animal homeopathic medicines. Camphor can help when teats are heavily swollen, but rubbing the teats with ice or a cold cloth (moisten and freeze) can also help relieve the pain. Feed the female less than usual, and make sure she gets enough attention and extra exercise.

Preparing to breed

If you do plan to breed a litter of puppies, you must first wait for your female to be physically and mentally ready. Be meticulous with your preparations and start searching for a suitable mate well in advance of the bitch's season. If your female is registered, and has passed all the health checks (see the chapter Health), a breed club will you help to find a stud dog. If you plan to mate your bitch with a dog that has not been listed by the breeding club it is important you consider the following before you make your choice:

- Do not pick a dog without a pedigree.
- Ensure that the owner has the necessary paperwork confirming that he does not have any inherited defects.
- Observe the dog's character and temperament and look for characteristics that will reinforce the positive qualities of your bitch.
- Never breed from two animals of extremes together. If both parents are hyperactive, for example, there is a high chance that this undesirable trait will be even stronger in their offspring.

* Never breed from a Dobermann with inherited or congenital defects.

The owner of the dog will generally ask for a cover fee for the mating, though occasionally, if they are particularly taken with the match they may ask for a puppy from the litter in lieu of payment.
Before mating your bitch, check that she is free of any parasites (external and internal). She must be fit, not overweight and vaccinated against all the usual diseases. If you want strong, healthy puppies, the mother-to-be must be in the best possible condition. As soon as the female shows the first signs of being on heat, make an appointment with the owner of the male for the first mating attempt. In most cases, after the first attempt the bitch is brought to the dog again after two or three days to ensure the mating is a success.
It is important to be aware that accompanying a bitch through pregnancy, birth and the first eight to twelve weeks afterwards is a time-consuming affair. Don't expect to get much sleep, or time to yourself during your litter's first few weeks of life.

Pregnancy

It is often difficult to tell if a bitch is pregnant at first, and it usually only after about four weeks that you can feel the pups in her womb. At this point her she will start to put on weight, her teats will swell up and her behaviour will usually begin to change. The average pregnancy lasts 63 days, and costs the bitch more and more in terms of energy. In the initial stages of pregnancy she should be fed her normal amount of food, but her nutritional needs increase in jumps during the second half of the pregnancy. Give her approximately fifteen percent more food each week from the fifth week on, as she will need extra energy and proteins during this phase of her pregnancy (see the chapter on Feeding)

During the last weeks you can give the bitch a concentrated food, rich in energy, such as dry puppy food. Divide this into several small portions per day, because she can no longer deal with large portions of food. Towards the end of the pregnancy, her energy needs can easily be one-and-a-half times more than usual.

After about seven weeks the mother will start to display signs of nesting, and will begin to look for a place to give birth to her pups. This might be her own basket or a special birthing box. Ensure that the basket or box is in a quiet place and is ready at least one week before the birth, to give the mother time to get used to it.

Birth

The average litter can be anything from three to nine puppies. The birth is usually straightforward, with little need for human intervention. Obviously if you suspect a problem it is essential that you contact your veterinarian immediately.

Suckling

After the birth, the mother starts to produce milk. The suckling period is very demanding as during the first three to four weeks the pups rely entirely on their mother's milk. During this time the bitch needs extra food and fluids - this can be up to three or four times the normal amount. If she is producing too little milk, you can supplement both the mother and her puppies with special puppy milk.

While the bitch is feeding the litter, divide the large quantity of food she needs into several small portions. Again, choose a concentrated, high-energy food and give her plenty of fresh drinking water – avoid cow's milk as this can upset the digestion and cause diarrhoea. Once the puppies are three weeks old you can start to supplement their diet with food. Start with specially designed starter food that complements the mother's milk, and can be easily digested. Start with one meal a day of starter food per week and gradually increase this.

When the puppies are seven weeks old, they should be fully weaned from their mother. At this point the bitch's milk production will slowly decrease, and her food intake should drop accordingly. Within a couple of weeks after weaning, the bitch's diet should have returned to normal (pre-pregnancy).

When you feed your puppies, make sure that each pup gets its fair share. If you feel that one pup is missing out, set it apart when feeding, but only do this as long as it is necessary. Try to get it eating with its brothers and sisters again as quickly as possible – as it is important each puppy learns to fend for itself in the pack. Over-eating is just as dangerous as under-eating, so increase the amount gradually. Watch for the growth and behaviour of the pups and regularly check that their stools are properly formed. Small hard stools can be a sign of malnutrition or lack of fluids. Stools that are too soft or runny are often caused by overfeeding.

Neutering and spaying

If you are sure you don't want to breed from your bitch it is essential you have her spayed. During spaying, the uterus is surgically removed, after which the bitch no longer goes into season and cannot become pregnant. The best age for spaying is about eighteen months, when the bitch is more or less fully-grown.

A male dog can also be neutered if you do not wish to keep him as a stud dog. During neutering the testicles are removed, which is a simple procedure and usually uncomplicated. There is no special age for neutering - where possible, wait until the dog is fully-grown.

Vasectomy is sufficient where it is only a case of making the dog infertile. In this case the dog keeps its sexual drive but can no longer reproduce.

Sports and shows

Dobermanns will not be happy with just going round the block once in a while, especially when they are young. They will get bored and will start to behave badly at home.

If you want to keep your young Dobermann happy, you will have to do something with him!
Choosing a Dobermann as a companion needs serious consideration, and means that you must be prepared to meet his physical and psychological needs.
Enthusiasts can actively work with their Dobermanns in many other ways. From tracking to sports, the possibilities are huge.

Behaviour and obedience

You can pick from a whole range of obedience training courses, beginning with a puppy course. Dobermanns usually enjoy this type of course. Their strong will to please means they want to perform the exercises as well as possible. After elementary obedience courses, you can train your dog for various behaviour and obedience diplomas.

Obedience

You can follow up on basic obedience training by trying to pass the Behaviour and Obedience diplomas, classes 1, 2 & 3, with increasing degrees of difficulty. This discipline is also practised in a competitive environment, and there are British, European and World Championships. Among other things the dog must walk on the lead, follow at foot off the lead, stay standing or sit or lie for a set time while his master walks away and is out of sight for several minutes. Tracking and retrieving is trained and tested almost to perfection.
The British form of Obedience goes a step further; the accent here is on perfect

performance of the set tasks. Highly intensive training is intended to make dog and master one unit, which, during the execution of several exercises, seems to be glued together. Obedience is only performed in competition, there are no diplomas.

Endurance test

This is primarily a European dog activity but dogs that have once learned to run alongside a bicycle usually enjoy it. And moreover, it's good for their muscle development and their body moves smoothly. Their muscles grow stronger without over-burdening their vulnerable joints. This is something that can be done along a canal towpath or along a -country trail – not on a public road though. Never let your Dobermann run beside the bike before he is one year old. Starting too young is bad for the development of his bones. Slowly build up the distance. Do not go out with a bike when it is too warm, never feed your dog shortly beforehand and do not go too far. Advanced Dobermann can take part in endurance competitions. The dog has to cover a distance of twenty kilometres beside the -bicycle, at a speed between fifteen and twenty kilometres per hour.

Road safety

Especially useful are road safety courses for dogs. Here, your Dobermann can learn a few obedience exercises and at the end of the course can show you how safely he conducts himself in traffic.

Traffic-training

All dogs that want to take part in training examinations, working trials, and competitions should be traffic-trained. This course is all about the handling of a dog in modern urban traffic. It consists of an obedience element (walking on the lead, walking free, sitting on command, staying combined with the "come!" command) and a practical element, which takes place on public roads and squares. The behaviour of the dog towards pedestrians and cyclists coming up from behind is examined, also his behaviour in

difficult traffic situations. Then one tests the behaviour of a dog alone for a short time and how he behaves towards other animals. At the end the dog has to pass some obedience exercises in traffic.

Agility

Agility is a form of dog sport that the Dobermann can enjoy to his heart's content. In this discipline, the dog has to run through a course. The art is to do this as fast as possible with as few penalty points as possible. The obstacles consist of a slalom, a seesaw, a tunnel, hurdles and a fence. The dog, spurred on by his master, must take all the obstacles correctly. The dog with the fastest time and the least penalty points is the -winner. The sport is demanding on dog and master and they both need to be very fit.

Flyball

The Dobermann will also enjoy this form of sport. In competitions, teams of four dogs face each other in the arena. The dogs must jump across four obstacles. They then reach a device with a narrow plank on the front. By pressing this plank with their paws they launch a (tennis) ball. They must then pick up the ball and bring it to their master as fast as possible. The first team to have all four balls is the winner.

Guard-dog training

This training consists of three elements: tracking, obedience and guard work (arrest work).

The guard work portion is both interesting and spectacular. However, the dog must be totally obedient before you can train him. People often think that arrest training makes a dog spiteful and untrustworthy, but the opposite is true. During guard service a dog must be extremely controlled, disciplined and easy to handle, and for this reason there are high demands in terms of obedience for guard service.

Tracker-dog training

In tracker-dog training, the dog must display sure tracking abilities and track a scent that is 1 mile long and at least three hours old. There are seven turns in the scent (matching the terrain). The trace is crossed by two distracting scents a good distance from each other. There are also seven obstacles at varying distances on the track.

Shows

If you plan to participate in dog shows with your Dobermann, it is important to accept that to your dog this activity can be of little or no interest. Visiting a show is highly recommended if you want to learn more about a certain breed. You will also be able to get into direct contact with breeders and other owners.

Dog showing is a very competitive sport, in which breeders and exhibitors invest a lot of time. Some breeders even dedicate their lives to this. There are lots of things to consider before entering in your first show. Firstly, you need to choose which shows to enter and what you need to achieve for the dog to be awarded a title.

Showing a dog requires a lot of planning, you cannot simply start preparing your dog a few weeks before the show. If you are serious about the show ring you must begin show training your puppy from a very young age. In order to become Champion your dog needs to have three Challenge Certificates awarded by three different judges. Of those three, at least one should be achieved when the dog is twelve months or older. Challenge Certificates can also be awarded to the best of each sex in a breed.

The British system allows a certain number of dogs per breed to be awarded the Challenge Certificate. The annual limit of Challenge Certificates to be awarded to representatives of a certain breed can be as many as 30 or as few as 6.
When the dogs enter the ring, the judge looks at them very carefully. Each dog is examined visually and physically by hand. The breed standards of most dog breeds contain remarks regarding the build – which the judge will be looking for in the show ring. The teeth will also be examined, as each breed standard will have its own notes regarding an undershot jaw or scissor bite. It is understandable that the judge will need to feel the dog in order to fully compare it to the breed standard. The breed standards also contain notes on gait and movement, which is why the judge will also need to see your dog move. Judges also pay attention to the carriage of the dog's head and tail.

Ringcraft classes are a fantastic way to learn how to prepare yourself and your dog for the show ring.
The classes are usually very sociable events, where training is combined with lots of fun.

Even if you do not plan to follow a showing career with your dog, it may still be a good idea to take it to a course. Your dog will learn to socialise with people that it does not know and with other dogs. It will also learn to walk on the lead properly without being distracted.
Some clubs that run ringcraft classes also organise friendly unofficial shows and Companion Dog Shows for their members once in a while.

Types of Shows

There are many different types of shows. Here is a brief overview:
Single Breed Shows (for one breed only, organised by a breed club)
Companion Dog Shows (for charitable causes)
Open Shows
Championship Shows (the most prestigious shows).

Your dog must look very smart for the show ring. The judge will not be impressed if your dog's coat is not clean and his paws are dirty. Nails must be clipped and the teeth must be free of plaque.
The dog must also be free from parasites and ailments. Judges also dislike badly behaved dogs, or anxious or nervous dogs.
Get in touch with a breed club if you want to know more about dog shows.

Don't forget!
If you're planning to take your dog to a club or show you need to be well prepared. Don't forget the following:

For yourself:
- Show documents
- Food and drink
- Clip for the catalogue number
- Chairs for an outdoor show

For your dog:
- Food and water (and bowls)
- Dog blanket and bed
- Show lead
- Reward treats
- Grooming equipment
- A benching chain and collar

Parasites

All dogs are vulnerable to various sorts of parasites. Parasites are tiny creatures that live off another animal (the host), feeding on blood, skin and other body substances. There are two main types; internal parasites, which live within their host animal's body (tapeworm and roundworm for example) and external parasites which live on the animal's exterior, usually in its coat (fleas, lice and ticks), but also in its ears (ear mites).

Fleas

Fleas feed on a dog's blood. They not only cause itching and skin problems, but can also carry infections such as tapeworm and in large numbers they can cause anaemia. Dogs can also become allergic to a flea's saliva, which can cause serious skin conditions. It is important to treat your dog against fleas, and in order for treatment to be effective do not just treat the dog, but also his surroundings. For treatment of the animal, there are various medicines: drops for the neck, drops to put in food, flea collars, long-life sprays and flea powders. There are various sprays in pet shops that can be used to eradicate fleas in the dog's immediate surroundings (including the car). Choose a spray that kills both adult fleas and their larvae. Fleas can also affect other pets, which should also be treated at the same time. When spraying a room, cover any aquarium or fishbowl, as if the spray reaches the water, it can be fatal for your fish! Your vet and pet shop will have a wide range of flea treatments and can advise you on this subject.

Ticks

Ticks are small, spider-like parasites that feed on the blood of the animal or person they have settled on. A tick looks like a tiny, grey-coloured leather bag with eight feet. When it has sucked itself full, it can easily increase to five to ten times its original size and becomes darker in colour. Dogs usually fall victim to ticks in bushes, woods or long grass.

Ticks not only irritate through blood sucking, but they can also carry a number of serious diseases. This is especially applicable in Mediterranean countries, where ticks can be infected with blood parasites. In the UK these diseases are fortunately less common, but Lyme disease, which can also affect humans, has reached our shores as well. Your vet can prescribe a special treatment if you are planning to take your dog to southern Europe. It is important to fight ticks as effectively as possible so check your dog regularly, especially when it has been running free in woods and bushes. Your dog can also wear an anti-tick collar.
Removing a tick is simple with a pair of tick tweezers. Grip the tick with the tweezers very close to the dog's skin, and carefully pull it out. You can also grip the tick between your fingers and by using a turning movement, pull it carefully out. You must disinfect the spot where the tick had been, using iodine to prevent infection. Never soak the tick in alcohol, ether or oil. In a shock reaction the tick may discharge the infected contents of its stomach into the dog's skin and infect your dog.

Flea

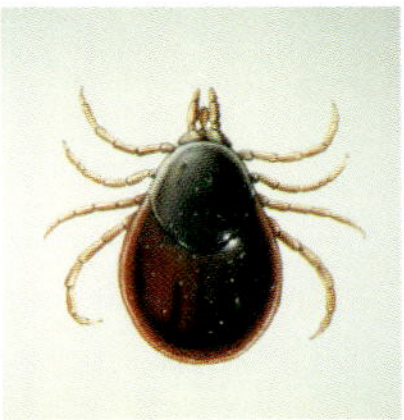

Tick

Puppy mange

Puppy mange, or "Demodex", affects almost all young dogs but does not cause problems for each one of them. The dog has little or no irritation, but some bald patches will appear on the head, neck and forepaws. A vet can often take biopsies of the skin to examine under the microscope and establish whether it is a case of puppy mange. Sometimes bacteria may play a major role and pussy blisters appear. Treatment consists of washing the dog with a substance that kills mites; of course this has to be done with the support of a vet.

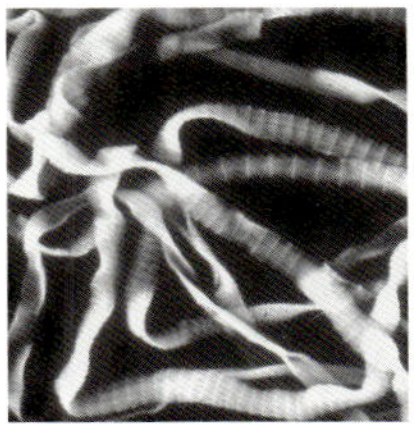

Tapeworm

Roundworm

Worms

Dogs can suffer from various types of worm, the most common being tapeworm and roundworm. Tapeworm causes diarrhoea and a poor general condition. With a tapeworm infection you can sometimes find small pieces of the worm around the dog's anus or on its bed. In this case, the dog must be wormed immediately. You should also check your dog for fleas, which carry the tapeworm infection.
Roundworm is a condition that reoccurs regularly and causes problems such as diarrhoea, loss of weight and stagnated growth, particularly in younger dogs - you may see evidence of the infestation in your dog's faeces.
Puppies are commonly infected through their mother's milk. Your vet can prescribe medicines to prevent roundworm. In serious cases the pup becomes thin, but with a swollen belly, he may vomit up spaghetti like tendrils of the worms. A puppy must be treated against worms every two weeks from the third week after birth, until he is three months old. At this point the puppy can be treated every three months until he is a year old. Adult dogs should be treated every six months. If your dog is obviously infested you should treat him immediately.

Health

This section looks at the ailments and disorders that specifically affect the Dobermann.

Breed-specific conditions

Check the parent dogs' papers to ensure they were free of Hip Dysplasia (HD) and hereditary eye conditions.
The breeding clubs try to keep their members informed about any health issues that might be useful to know when breeding Dobermanns.

Hip Dysplasia (HD)

Many breeds are vulnerable to HD. Hip Dysplasia is an abnormality of the hip joints in the hind quarters, whereby the socket of the hip joint and the head of the upper thigh do not match properly. This causes an inflammation and bone tumours, which can be very painful. Until recently, it was assumed that HD was primarily caused by genetic factors. Recent investigations, however, indicate that while genetic factors certainly play a role in terms of a dog's susceptibility to HD, external factors such as food quality and exercise appear at least equally important. Limit the chance of HD as far as possible by giving your dog ready-made food of a good brand, and never add any supplements! Make sure your dog does not get too fat. A puppy should be somewhat protected from HD in its first year. Do not let it romp too much with other dogs, chase sticks and balls too wildly or run up and down stairs. These kinds of games cause the pup to make abrupt and risky movements, which can overburden its soft joints. One important but under-estimated factor behind HD is the floor in your home. Parquet and tiled floors are much too slippery for a young dog. Regular slipping can cause complications that promote HD. If you have a smooth floor, it is advisable to lay blankets or old carpets in places the dog uses regularly. Let it spend lots of time in the garden, as grass is a perfect surface to run on. The breed associations try to keep control by strictly testing potential breeding animals. An X-ray examination for HD is therefore recommended to all animals intended for breeding. The breeding stock needs to have a score sheet from the BVA, which the breeders should be happy to show you for both sire and dam.

Hereditary Eye Conditions

PHTVL/PHPV

This abbreviation stands for Persistent Hyperplastic Tunica Vasculosa Lentis / Persistent Hyperplastic Primary Vitreous.
It is a rare congenital eye ¬abnormality. It is caused by a disturbance in ¬develop¬ment whereby remnants of the embryonic blood vessel coat of the lens that feeds the eye with nutrients during pregnancy. The condition is graded from "suspicious", grade 1, to "serious", grade 6.

PHTVL: Persistent Hyperplastic Tunica Vasculosa Lentis

PHTVL refers to the persistence of the embryonic vascular system of the lens. This condition is an eye anomaly that has been found in many animals as well as in human beings. This eye condition results from a failure of the embryological, primary vitreous and hyaloid vasculature to regress.

PHPV: Persistent Hyperplastic Primary Vitreous

PHPV also refers to the persistence of the embryonic vascular system of the lens. This condition is an eye anomaly that has been found in many animals as well as in human beings. This eye condition results from a failure of the embryological, primary vitreous and hyaloid vasculature to regress.

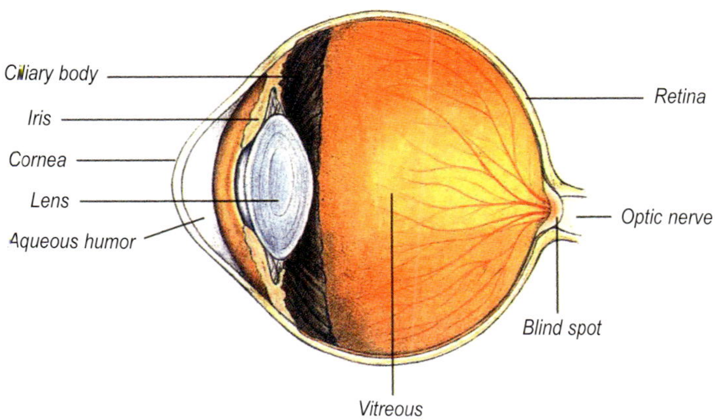

Cross-sectional view of the eye

This is a type op cataract, however up to now nobody knows the mode of inheritance. Even if the tested dog is free from PHTVL and PHPV, it might pass on the defective gene to its offspring.
It is possible to screen a litter for PHPV from the age of 6 weeks onwards. PHPV is a congential (there from birth) defect and if a puppy is screened at the age of 6 weeks and declared unaffected it will not develop this condition later in his life.
If buying a puppy it is advisable to seek a puppy that has been screened, as you can then be sure that your puppy will not be affected by PHPV. Anyone breeding a litter is strongly advised to take the whole litter for screening before sale.

Entropion and ectropion

Ectropion

With ectropion the eyelid is turned away from the eye. The eyelids do not close properly over the eyeball and the cornea is no longer properly protected. Contamination can easily get in causing strong irritation. The eyes become infected and discharge pus. This can cause serious damage to the cornea and eventually even cause blindness. Ectropion can be corrected surgically.

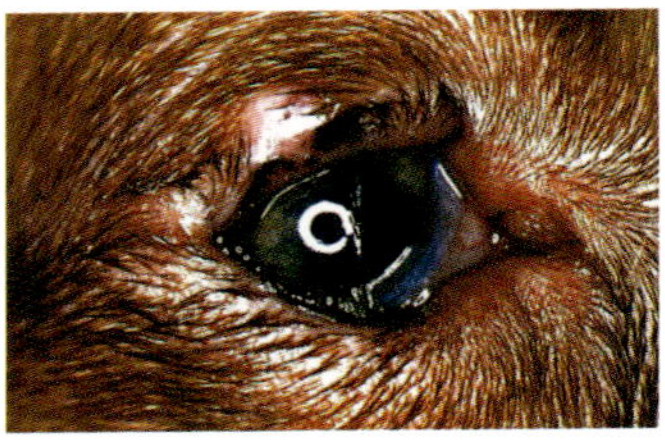
Entropion

Entropion

These are genetic conditions affecting the eyelids. With entropion the eyelids are curled inwards, with ectropion outwards.
With entropion the eyelashes contact the eyeball, cause irritation and lead to red, watering eyes. The dog often walks with its eyes squinting, and in serious cases it will keep the eyes completely closed. If no action is taken, the cornea takes on a bluish glow.
If one leaves the condition untreated, the cornea can become infected and can even be destroyed, leaving the dog blind. So it is vital that you visit a veterinarian whenever your dog seems to have problems with its eyes. A veterinarian will often administer vitamin A drops in these cases, or a lotion to protect the cornea. Sometimes the vet may find it necessary to tack the eye. Entropion can be corrected surgically.

Progressive Retina Atrophy (P.R.A.)

Also known as PRA. Sometimes referred to as "night blindness", which is a misnomer because the blindness caused by this disease is eventually total. In the early stages, the

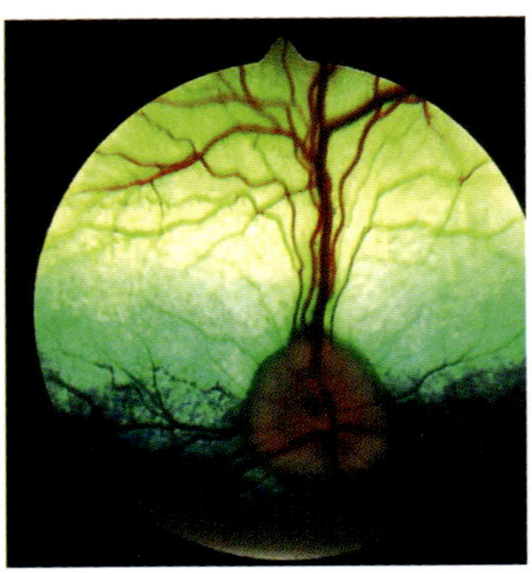
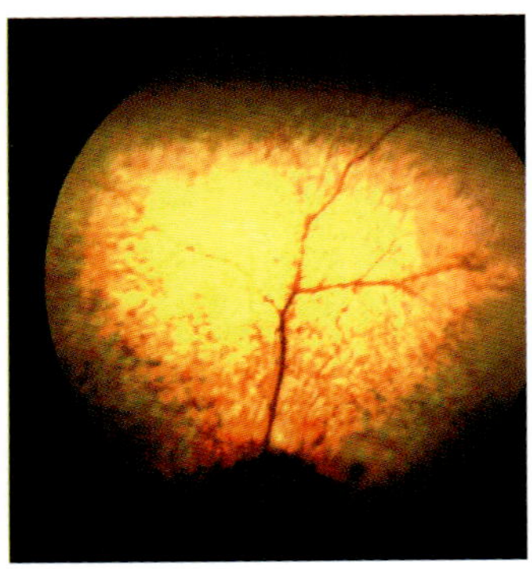
Left: normal retina

Right: PRA

dog's vision is impaired at night and eventually becomes worse in daylight and dim light conditions. Ultimately, the dog becomes completely blind as both eyes are affected. This condition is an inherited one with both parents being carriers. A screening test is available and can be performed by a veterinary ophthalmologist. CERF (Canine Eye Registration Foundation) will certify eyes for 12 months from the date of evaluation. This condition exists in quite a number of breeds.

Blood disorder

Von Willebrand's disease (vWD)

This is a bleeding disease characterized by excessive bleeding time due to delayed clotting. vWD is very often seen in conjunction with hypothyroidism. When there is a blood test available, which identifies carriers, affected and clear animals, though the test is sensitive to a number of criteria and hormone levels that affect scores. Research is close to develop a DNA test that will be much more effective in giving absolute information.

Dilated Cardiomyopathy

This heart disease is rather common in giant breeds. In this condition we see a weakness of the heart muscles.
One of the more common conditions is dilated cardiomyopathy or DCM, which causes the heart muscle to become weak so that eventually the heart is unable to pump effectively. This can take many years meaning that a dog can have a heart disease for a long time before symptoms will be visible. However, eventually it results in the appearance of signs of heart failure, such as weakness, exercise intolerance, difficulty breathing, coughing and weight loss.
At the moment it is possible to make a DNA-test for this condition.

Hypothyroidism

Canine Hypothyroidism is the most commonly diagnosed hormonal disease found in dogs. The term hypothyroidism simply means the underproduction of thyroxin, the hormone produced by the thyroid gland.
The thyroid gland is located on the trachea (wind pipe) of the dog, just below the voice box. It exerts its influence on the dog's body by producing and releasing thyroxin into the blood stream. This hormone, and thus, the thyroid gland itself, is very important in controlling growth and development and maintaining normal protein, carbohydrate and lipid metabolism of the dog.
Hypothyroidism usually occurs between the ages of two to six years. The most common sign is an increase in body weight. Lethargy and some form of skin disease (i.e., thin coat, loss of hair, dandruff, oily skin, increased scratching) are also common signs of Hypothyroidism.

The treatment is through thyroid hormone supplementation given orally once or twice a day. Usually thyroid supplementation improves the clinical signs associated with the disease within four to six weeks. All the clinical signs of hypothyroidism are reversible, once treatment is started.
The disease has a genetic component, and available data suggest that the trait is recessive.

Cervical Spondylo Myelopathy (Wobbler's Syndrome)

This is suspected to be an inherited condition and it does not often occur when a dog is older than 12 months.
The dog suffers from spinal cord compression caused by cervical vertebral instability or from a malformed spinal canal. Extreme symptoms are paralysis of the limbs (front, hind or all 4). Neck pain with extension and flexion may or may not be present. Surgical therapy is hotly debated and in some surgically treated cases, clinical recurrence has been identified.

Albinism

"White coated" and "white factored" Dobermans should NOT be bred. These dogs are *TYROSINASE POSITIVE ALBINOS*. In 1996, the AKC established a tracking system (the letter "Z" will be part of the registration number) allowing breeders to identify the normal coloured Dobermans that may carry the albinistic gene. A list with all dogs tracing back to Shebah's (the first Albino Doberman registered) parents is available from the DPCA. All breeders should require an AKC certified pedigree with colours to check that "white coated" and "white factored" dogs are not present in the pedigree of the dog or bitch to be mated.

It is important to know the status before breeding with a dog or bitch - clinically affected dogs, dogs exhibiting symptoms for any of these conditions, should NOT be used for breeding. The text is intended as an aid to those seeking health information and should not be used to form a diagnosis replacing regular veterinary care by one's own veterinarian.

Diseases caused by viruses and other organisms

Pseudo rabies

Pseudo rabies or Aujeszky's disease is actually a disease found in pigs. The virus is transferred to other animals when they eat raw infected pork. The disease affects the central nervous system, and a dog, which has been infected with the virus becomes restless, apathetic, nervous and loses its appetite. Aujeszky's disease progresses incredibly quickly: the animal will become paralysed and die within a week. There is no cure, so never feed dogs (or other pets) raw or ill cooked pork.

Corona

Corona is a viral disease, the symptoms of which are vomiting and diarrhoea. This disease looks like a parvo virus infection, but is less severe in its progress. Besides the symptoms listed under parvo virus, other symptoms include damage to the mucous membranes, which manifests itself in eye and nose discharge. The disease is spread via faeces.

Hepatitis

Hepatitis is a highly infectious liver disease. The virus is found in both dogs and foxes. The noticeable symptoms vary widely. Approximately one week after infection, the body temperature increases, after which the dog's temperature starts to fluctuate.

The dog remains lively during the first few days, but this quickly changes. Symptoms include; coughing and an inflamed throat, moist eyes and a lack of appetite, sometimes in combination with vomiting and/or diarrhoea. The dog's eyes will cloud over and the virus is spread via the urine of infected dogs. As infected dogs urinate in parks and against trees, the disease spreads very quickly.

Hepatitis symptoms vary from light fever to a very serious liver infection. If the disease is treated at an early stage, there is a chance of full recovery, if the liver is infected, however, the fever will run very high and the dog will no longer eat. Invariably, if the disease reaches this stage the dog will die. Hepatitis can cause young dogs and puppies to die very suddenly.

Hepatitis is not always easy to diagnose, as the symptoms are very similar to those of Carré's disease.

Carré's disease
This disease is caused by a virus and is highly infectious. The severity of the first symptoms, a runny nose and a cough, is often underestimated and shortly after this the dog will develop a fever, followed by a lack of appetite, vomiting and/or diarrhoea. Furthermore, the dog will suffer from an inflamed throat and discharge from the nose and eyes, spasms and cramps. A young dog may suddenly become severely ill. The virus causes inflammation in the intestines, but also leads to meningitis. Many dogs do not survive this disease, and the dogs that do survive, often suffer permanent nerve damage, or a 'tick'. Many dogs have behavioural disorders, which they did not have before the infection, e.g. orientation problems. The disease is spread via saliva, urine and faeces.

Rabies
This viral disease is fatal to humans and dogs. The virus enters the body when saliva from an infected animal reaches a wound of a hitherto healthy animal. It spreads via nerves to the brain, and will eventually kill the animal. Luckily, rabies does not exist in the UK, but if you are planning to take your dog abroad, you should have it vaccinated against rabies. Rabies is spread via the saliva (bites) of foxes, badgers and other animals.

Kennel cough
The kennel cough syndrome is caused by a number of different microorganisms: Para-influenza virus, Bordetella and others.
The disease usually spreads when dogs are kept in close proximity to each other, such as in a kennel, dog hotel, at a show or at a training class. The symptoms of this respiratory problem are a harsh, rough cough and occasionally damage to the lungs.
Dogs do not usually become severely ill from kennel cough, but you must have your dog treated by a vet. Cough medicine (thyme syrup) can help to soften the mucous membranes and a holiday in a place with lots of fresh air can do wonders. If you are going to leave your dog in a boarding kennel, it is best (and usually also required) to have your dog vaccinated against kennel cough. You should have your dog vaccinated against this obnoxious cough approximately four weeks before it goes in to kennels. The disease is spread via the breath.

Parvo virus
Parvo virus is a highly infectious viral disease and an infected dog rarely survives. The virus is spread via the faeces of an infected dog, when a healthy dogs sniffs at these

faeces, it immediately becomes infected. The virus penetrates the intestines, where it causes serious inflammation. Within a very short time, the dog will suffer bloody diarrhoea, may vomit blood, become drowsy, develop a fever and is suddenly very seriously ill.
The dog will usually refuse food or water and can therefore dehydrate. Treatment primarily consists of administering large amounts of fluid intravenously, however most dogs die within 48 hours of the first symptoms. In puppies, an infection with parvo virus can cause cardiac arrest, but today puppies are usually vaccinated against parvo virus very early in life. Puppies which have survived the disease may unfortunately die very suddenly later in life due to angina.

Weil's disease
Weil's disease (leptospirosis) is a disease caused by microorganisms. Dogs are most commonly infected in spring or autumn, and in younger dogs, the disease can often be fatal. A dog swimming in contaminated water might contract bacteria via the mucous membranes or tiny wounds on the skin, and from there, the bacteria gathers in the liver and kidneys. The symptoms include; high fever, drowsiness and muscle pain. Furthermore, the dog suffers from a lack of appetite, vomiting and is very thirsty.
The dog may also suffer from nosebleeds, dark urine and sometimes yellow fever. The disease is spread via the urine of infected rats and dogs.
Humans can also be infected through dogs or rats.

First aid for dogs

When your dog becomes injured or ill, the time that passes before professional veterinary help is available can be crucial. Whatever you do or do not do in this time can save your pet's life.
Remember that the first aid you apply is only intended to gain control over acute emergency situations. Your dog may have suffered internal injuries, which you are not aware of, therefore always take your dog to a veterinarian for examination!

If you are in any doubt about anything, ask your vet for advice. Applying medical aid to an animal always has one complication - communication with the patient – as you cannot explain to a dog that you are trying to help it and lessen its pain. A seriously injured animal is scared and in a lot of pain, and will therefore often try to escape or to attack its helper(s). It is essential that you gently restrain the dog so that you do not get hurt. At the same time, you must make it clear to the animal, through a firm but friendly approach, that you are sympathetic, but in control of the situation. Keep talking calmly and frequently address the animal by its name, the tone of your voice and the sound of his name will have a calming, relaxing effect. Persuade the dog to sit or lie on a table as this makes it more difficult for him to escape, and makes treatment easier for you.

Not all cases requiring first aid are the same, as one situation may be more severe than another and may require quicker intervention. There is a fixed order of treatment, from very severe to less severe. It is therefore very important to stick to this order when treating wounds and conditions. In the overview on the next page you will see which life functions must be restored first, before you begin treating the next function.

Order of treatment

1. Respiration
2. Heart function
3. Blood vessels
4. Shock
5. Poisoning
6. Fractures
7. Digestive tract
8. Other injuries

1. Respiration

Together with the heart function, breathing is an animal's most important vital function. Breathing allows oxygen to be absorbed into the body, which is necessary to allow the organs and tissues to function properly. If the body becomes deficient in oxygen for too long, the organs and tissues will quickly become damaged and will eventually die off. If respiration stops, the animal is in acute danger. A dog with breathing difficulties often stretches its neck out and tries to inhale air with all its might; the mucous membranes of the tongue and the eyes turn blue and the animal will become unconscious after a while. If your dog is lying absolutely still and you cannot see anything on first sight, check the breathing by laying your hand or a few fingers on the chest: you should feel it moving up and down.

If your dog is struggling to breathe, take it in to the fresh air immediately. Try to discover what is the cause of the breathing difficulties as quickly as possible and eliminate it as soon as you can. Remove any possibly obstructing objects from the neck (collars, flea collars), and check that no objects are stuck in the throat or windpipe. In some cases you can apply a short thrust on the chest and push the object out with the air from the lungs. Applying pressure on the outside of the throat will also sometimes help.

If the dog is choking on water, you need to lift it up by its back legs with the head hanging down. This allows the fluid to drain from the lungs. Then push on the chest a few times to remove the last remaining fluid from the lungs.

If the dog is still experiencing breathing difficulties you will need to apply mouth-to-mouth resuscitation to your dog. Try to take the victim to the veterinarian as quickly as possible, continuing to apply mouth-to-mouth resuscitation during the journey.

Possible causes of respiratory problems:
- Too little oxygen in the environment (insufficient ventilation, plastic bag, box).
- Water, gas or smoke in the lungs (drowning, carbon monoxide, fire).
- Swallowed objects, swelling of the mucous membranes in the respiratory tract (asthmatic attack, inflammation), swelling of the tongue (wasp's sting).
- Restricted throat (collar, flea collar).
- Damage to the diaphragm, broken ribs.
- Damaged lungs.
- Suffocating on food (through fright) or vomit.

Loss of consciousness
A dog can lose consciousness for a number of reasons; epilepsy, a heavy blow, brain haemorrhaging and poisoning are just a few examples. If your dog loses consciousness you should always consider it an emergency, in which case you need to act as follows:
- Get someone to notify the vet straight away.
- Lay the dog on his side, as long as you cannot detect a wound there, with the paws pointing away from the body. The head needs to lie in a higher position than the rest of the body.
- Check the pulse. If necessary, apply heart massage.
- Check the respiration. If necessary, apply mouth-to-mouth resuscitation.
- When the dog is breathing again, pull its tongue out of its mouth and remove any food remains.
- Do not give the dog food or water.
- Keep the animal warm with a blanket.

2. Heart function

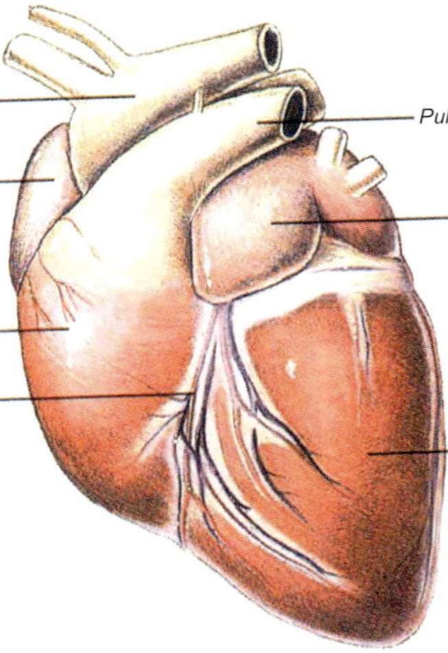

Above: schematic representation of the heart

Below: cross-sectional view of the heart

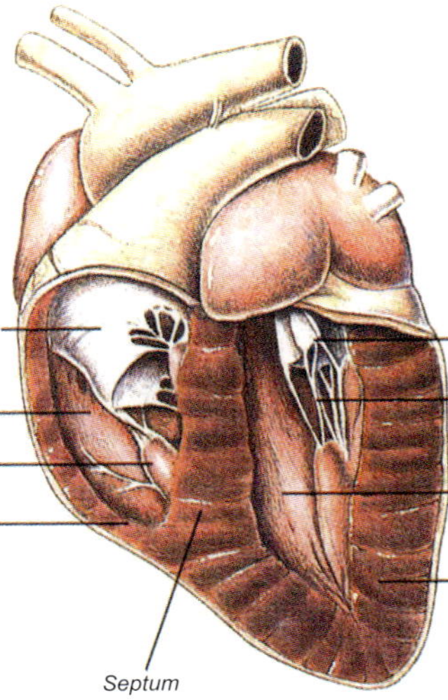

A dog can suffer from a heart attack, but not every heart attack results in a cardiac arrest.
Some causes of heart attacks include drowning, suffocation, poisoning, severe allergic reaction, trauma or electric shock.
Symptoms include pain, shortness of breath, nausea or vomiting and dizziness.
Do not just assume that the symptoms will pass, if you suspect heart failure, you must take your dog to the veterinarian as quickly as possible.

3. Blood vessels

Bleeding

A dog can become injured and lose blood. In the case of serious blood loss, the animal may die. How much blood is lost and how quickly depends on the size of the wound, but also on the type of blood vessel. We differentiate between three types of bleeding, depending on the type of blood vessel injured:

Capillary bleeding

This is a fairly harmless bleed; however, it does need to be treated. The wound is not deep (often only a scrape) and there is little loss of blood. Disinfect the wound well, and briefly press it closed with some gauze. You often do not even need to dress it.

Venous bleeding

In this type of bleeding the blood streams out of the wound steadily and is dark red in colour. This is because the blood is flowing towards the heart through the veins and is low in oxygen. Clean the wound well with a disinfectant tissue or sterile gauze soaked in boiled water and then dress it. Take your dog to the veterinarian straight away, they will again disinfect the wound thoroughly and stitch it if necessary.

Arterial bleeding

This is a very serious type of bleed, which can be fatal for your dog. The blood gushes out of the wound intermittently and is light red in colour. This is because it comes straight from the heart and contains a lot of oxygen. The dog loses a lot of blood in a very short time, and you therefore need to act very quickly.

- Hold the dog with a restraining grip and try to calm it. Use your voice to prevent it losing consciousness.
- First check respiration and pulse, and then try to stop the bleeding.
- Place the injured part at a higher angle than the rest of the body.
- Put sterile gauze or a clean cloth on the wound, and exert pressure with the palm of your hand, so that the blood vessel is squeezed tight. If necessary, put some extra gauze or cotton wool on the wound and exert more pressure. On spots where the skin is loose (lips, cheeks, scruff), tightly push the wound edges together in your fist.
- Once the bleeding has stopped, put

a thick layer of cotton wool on the gauze or cloth. Bandage the wound with a tight bandage. Keep on exerting pressure.
- Take the dog to the veterinarian as quickly as possible.

Major bleeding at the foot or tail can be stopped by exerting pressure on one of the so-called pressure points with your finger. These are points where the blood vessels run closely under the skin and are easily squeezed tight.

If you cannot manage to stop arterial bleeding in the manner described above, you can apply a tourniquet as a last resort. A tourniquet must never be applied around the neck or head. After applying a tourniquet, take the dog to the veterinarian as quickly as possible. Be aware that a dog can go into shock as a result of serious bleeding.

Minor cut and stab wounds:
- Hold the dog in a restraining grip. It will probably try to resist.
- Wash your hands thoroughly and where possible use sterile material from a first aid kit.
- Remove any hairs that might be in the wound: dampen them with clean water, stroke them out of the wound and cut them off close to the skin. Examine the depth of the wound.
- Rinse the wound clean with a mild disinfectant, which is dissolved in water. You can also dissolve two teaspoons of salt in a litre of tap water. Try to gently rub open small deep stab wounds.
- Wash the skin around the wound with diluted disinfectant. Cover the wound with sterile gauze, to prevent suds getting in, and rinse with plenty of clean water afterwards.
- In graze wounds, in particular, there may be a lot of dirt in the skin. Remove it with a cotton bud or a corner of a clean cloth – but be very careful when doing this!
- Dab the wound dry with a clean, non-fluffy cloth.
- Put disinfectant salve on the wound and bandage it.
- Change the dressing every day and pay close attention to possible wound infections.
- If a scab has formed, you need to prevent the dog removing it. Keep the wound edges supple with Vaseline or cod-liver oil salve.

Major cuts or skin parts missing:
- In these cases your first aid attempts must be directed towards getting the animal to the veterinarian as quickly as possible, and to prevent the situation from worsening.
- The dog might be in a lot of pain, if necessary, apply a restraining grip.
- Remove any large objects, such as splinters, stones and twigs, from the wound. Do not remove objects that have deeply penetrated the skin. If they stick out of the wound, cut them off above the skin.
- Soak a clean cloth in a solution of two teaspoons of salt in one litre of water. Lay the wet cloth on the wound and secure it with tape or bandage clamps.
- Keep the cloth wet with the saline solution during the transport to the veterinarian.
- Make sure that the animal cannot lick or bite the wound.
- A deep wound needs to be stitched by a vet as soon as possible. This will speed up the healing process.

A dog can also suffer wounds when the skin is still intact. Examples of this are bruises or haemorrhages. You can treat these by applying ice cubes wrapped in a tea towel. Your

dog can also suffer more serious, internal damage. Symptoms include lightening of the mucous membranes and/or bloody discharge or slime from the nose. In the case of internal injuries, you must not move your dog or allow it to drink - call a vet straight away!

Burns

The skin is a very important organ for any animal. It protects the body against damaging external influences by giving it the right signals (e.g. it is warm). The skin also sends signals from the animal to its surroundings, e.g. hairs standing up. The coat is covered with aromatic substances, sweat and fats, which come from the skin. Finally the skin also regulates the body's temperature and the dog's water balance; it makes sure that the body does not dehydrate in a warm environment. Burns can have serious consequences, especially when major parts of the skin have been affected. In these cases the skin can no longer fulfil its vital functions.
In the case of burns you always need to apply first aid. The animal will be in a lot of pain and will need to be examined by a vet as soon as possible. He will judge if the dog can be saved. Whether a dog can recover depends on the percentage of skin damaged and on how deeply the burn has penetrated the skin.

You can try to prevent the condition worsening by thoroughly cooling off the animal as quickly as possible. Proceed as follows:

- Cool the burnt part of the skin with cold water as soon as possible (if necessary by dumping the dog in a pond or bucket). The cold not only alleviates the pain, but also cools the skin, which prevents deeper skin layers being seriously damaged.

- You need to cool off the dog for at least ten minutes. Carefully dab dry the area around the affected spot, but do not touch the wound: the risk of infection is too great.
- Do not put any salve or grease on the wound.
- Cover the wound with a clean cloth soaked in a solution of two teaspoons of salt in a litre of water. Keep the cloth damp with this solution during your drive to the veterinarian.
- Give the dog small amounts of water - if it can still swallow - over short intervals (the mucous membranes of the throat and mouth may have been affected by the smoke).
- Burnt skin can no longer contain body warmth, which means that the dog may shake because of the cold. Keep it warm with a blanket.
- Even if your dog is obviously in a lot of pain, never give it painkillers or sedatives of your own accord.

Bite wounds

Occasionally, dogs can get bitten by a feral animal, such as a fox or a stray cat or dog. First of all, you should clean the wound with disinfectant, then take your dog to the veterinarian as quickly as possible for further treatment.

4. Shock

Shock is not actually a condition as such, but can be the result of serious injuries combined with severe blood loss, a bad fright or pain. An injured animal may also become stressed by your attempts to treat it, which can also easily lead to shock. Preventing shock is actually more important than treating it, as a shocked animal has too little blood pumped through the body. If this continues for long, tissues and organs do not receive enough oxygen, so they start to die. If the brain gets insufficient oxygen, the animal will lose consciousness.

In cases where there is a real chance of the dog going into shock, you need to act as follows.

Free the respiratory tract by pulling the tongue a little out of the mouth - checking first for any objects in the throat or mouth. If necessary, apply mouth-to-mouth resuscitation and/or heart massage and stop any bleeding. An animal with very high fever or heatstroke (sunstroke) needs to be cooled with cold, wet cloths applied to the head and neck. Bring the dog into quiet, dark surroundings and make sure that the head is positioned a little higher than the rest of the body. If the dog has gone into shock keep him warm with a blanket and maybe with a hot water bottle (maximum 45°C). Alternatively, in the case of sunstroke, keep the dog cool.

If the animal can still drink, give it small amounts of water. Never offer it anything to drink if there is any suspicion of internal damage. Take your dog to the veterinarian as quickly as possible, they will put him on a drip to stabilise the blood pressure.

Causes of shock:

- Cardiac arrest
- Severe bleeding
- Dehydration
- Bad fright
- Severe pain
- Poisoning
- Allergies
- Brain trauma
- Serious burns
- Severe stress
- Malignant tumours
- Septicaemia
- Heatstroke
- High fever
- Prolonged vomiting/ diarrhea

Speedy actions can prevent your dog actually going into shock! If you see the following symptoms, you need to apply first aid immediately:

- Weak, irregular pulse
- Hectic, superficial breathing
- Cold ears and feet
- Pale skin (abdomen and inner thighs) and pale mucous membranes (mouth, eyes) and ears
- Apathy and anxiety

Epileptic seizure

A seizure can be of varying length. The dog will fall over and stay lying in an abnormal position with convulsions. It may urinate, drool or have widened pupils.

After a seizure your dog will be exhausted and gasping from the exertion and will be dull and uncoordinated. An epileptic fit looks very serious and can cause panic in anyone witnessing it, but with properly applied first aid, the whole situation is a lot less dramatic than it first looks. Therefore stay calm and proceed as follows:

- Carefully drag the dog by its back legs or body to a place where it cannot injure itself through its thrashing movements. For example, never leave it lying at the top of the stairs.
- Try to lessen the convulsions by putting a blanket or cloth over the animal and by surrounding it with cushions. This also decreases the risk of the animal injuring itself.
- Never try to apply a halter or hold the animal in a restraining grip and do not give your dog any food, water or medication.

- If necessary, apply mouth-to-mouth resuscitation, but watch your fingers when the dog starts breathing again.
- Allow the dog to come round in a calm, dark environment and stay and observe him for at least half an hour.
- If the seizures return within a short interval, you are facing an emergency situation. Take the animal to the veterinarian as soon as possible.

Heatstroke

A dog may be affected by heat, and this most often happens when the animal is left in a badly ventilated car. It cannot be stressed too often that a dog should never be left alone in a car in warm or sunny weather, even for a few minutes. Heatstroke can be recognised by the following symptoms: fast, jerky breathing, a glazed look and a body temperature of more than 40°C.

Take the dog to a shady, cool place and immerse it in a bucket or tub of cold water or hose it down. Cool off sparsely haired parts of the body, such as the belly, the elbows and the groin first. When the body temperature drops below 39°C you can start to dry the dog off and allow him small drinks of water at intervals of a few minutes. Take the dog to the veterinarian as soon as possible.

5. Poisoning

If an animal has been poisoned, it may develop a number of different symptoms. A poisoned dog will often have difficulty breathing, and will feel cold to touch as well as possibly losing consciousness. However, the dog may also start to shake and become hyperactive. Always remember that there is an increased chance of the dog going into shock.

Remove any remnants of the poison from its mouth or the skin with a cloth as quickly as possible. Try to find out what the poison is, and if possible take the package or whatever is left of the toxin to the veterinarian. This may be vital when it comes to determining the right antidote. How your dog is treated by the vet depends on the type of poison it has ingested.

If your dog has ingested something from the group of 'non-caustic' substances (see table), you need to make it vomit as quickly as possible. You can stimulate vomiting by placing a teaspoon of salt on the back of its tongue. Take a sample of

the vomit to the veterinarian. If the dog is unconscious, lay its head lower than the rest of the body as this allows the vomit to flow out of its mouth and prevents it from flowing into the lungs. If necessary, apply mouth-to-mouth resuscitation. If the animal cannot be taken to a vet immediately, it is best to wrap it in a blanket and to take it to a dark, quiet place. Sometimes packages of toxins contain information on which substances need to be administered as antidotes. If the dog has thrown up properly, you can give it a mix of milk and Norit. This is advisable if it will take some time before you can take your dog to the veterinarian.

If your pet has ingested a 'caustic' substance (see table), it must not throw up under any circumstances! The mucous membranes of the mouth, throat and gullet may have already been seriously damaged by the caustic toxin. If the toxin passes through them again, the damage will be more serious. Try to dilute the toxins in the digestive tract. In the case of a base toxin, give your dog vinegar or lemon juice. If your dog has ingested an acid, feed it soda or milk.

Non-caustic substances:
- Anti-freeze
- Bleach (chlorine)
- Pesticides:
  - Strychnine
  - Crimidine
- Lead (paint and roof covering)
- Insecticides:
  - Parathion
  - Dichlorvos
- Snail poison

Caustic substances:
- Base
  - Caustic Soda
  - Many paint or wallpaper strippers
- Petrol
- Paint thinner
- Acids
  - Battery acid
  - Hydrochloric acid

6. Fractures

Unfortunately, dogs quite regularly break or fracture bones. The prominent cause of fractures is road traffic accidents, but a fall from height, a bite by another animal or a gunshot wound may also lead to fractures. When applying first aid to fractures you need to be very careful, as the hard, sharp edges of the broken bone can easily damage tissues and organs.

Fractures can be differentiated into two groups. In closed fractures the skin has not been damaged and the fractured parts are therefore not exposed to the air. In open fractures the fractured parts break out of the skin through the wound. This type of fracture can have serious consequences, as the very sensitive bone marrow can become infected by bacteria. Such an infection can make an animal seriously ill and will slow down the healing process of the fracture.

An open fracture is obviously easy to diagnose. In the case of a closed fracture this is a little more difficult. There are, however, some symptoms which indicate a fracture: pain, swelling, loss of function in the broken limb, abnormal position of the bone, abnormal mobility of the broken limb and a grating sound during movement. When you have clearly diagnosed a fracture, you should proceed as follows:

- Hold your dog in a restraining grip and let it calm down as much as possible at the scene of the accident.
- Be aware of shock symptoms. They may occur if your dog is in a lot of pain.
- Make sure that the broken leg lies on top.
- Do not pull on the leg and make sure that the fracture is as still as possible.
- If the lower part of the leg is broken and if you need to transport the animal quite a distance, apply a preliminary splint. This can be a straight piece of wood, a piece of carton or a rolled-up newspaper. Carefully apply cotton wool or a thick cloth around the leg. Then apply the splints at the sides of the leg, so that the joints above and under the fracture can no longer move.
- Fasten the splints with tape or bandages, but do not pull them too tight. It is only a matter of immobilising the fracture for the time of transport, so that it does not move.
- Carefully push a blanket or board under the dog and lift the animal up. Make sure that it lies as quietly as possible.
- Take the animal to the veterinarian straight away.

In the case of an open fracture you need to make sure that the animal does not lick or scratch at the fracture. Put plenty of sterile gauze or a clean cloth onto the wound, so that no dirt can get into it. Do not put any salve or iodine onto it, as this only increases the risk of infection. The vet will need to treat an open fracture further.

7. Digestive tract

Vomiting

It is quite normal that dogs sometimes eat grass and throw up. They do this when their stomach bothers them as eating grass stimulates vomiting, which means that the dog discards its stomach contents.
If a dog throws up too often, something is definitely wrong. Throwing up can have different causes, such as infections, worms, eating too much, poisoning and metabolic disturbances. Take your dog to the veterinarian as quickly as possible if it is throwing up heavily, throwing up blood or if it has a swollen belly and a very ill appearance.

If your dog throws up regularly, but does not appear to be unwell generally you can wait and see if the symptoms disappear, feed easily digestible food and consult your vet if necessary. You sometimes need to feed your dog in the evening to prevent so-called 'bile vomiting' in the morning. You can buy special, easily digestible food at your pet shop or veterinarian for such cases. Divide the food into several portions per day, feeding every two to four hours for example, so the stomach gets the ideal opportunity to digest the food. Also make sure that your dog has plenty of fresh drinking water available. When the dog has stopped vomiting completely, you can carefully switch back to normal feeding. Start by replacing ten percent of the diet food with normal food. The next day replace twenty percent, and so on until the diet is one hundred percent normal food. If the problems have not disappeared, you need to contact a vet.

Diarrhoea

When your dog's faeces are soft or watery, it is suffering from diarrhoea. This is a symptom of a disturbed digestion, which can have several causes, such as infection, worms, eating bad or cold food or a sudden change in the diet. If the diarrhoea is bloody, or if it is combined with symptoms such as fever, vomiting and apathy, take your dog to the veterinarian as soon as possible.

If your dog is suffering from light diarrhoea without being ill in any other way, feed it an easily digestible diet to solve the problem. Your vet or pet shop will have special, easily digestible feeds. Divide the feed into several smaller portions per day and feed it until the symptoms disappear, then slowly go back to normal food. This is best done by replacing ten percent of the diet food by normal food daily until the diet is one hundred per cent normal food. Always contact your vet if the diarrhoea persists for more than a day or two.

8. Other injuries

Bruises

To control the swelling, you can cover a bruise with a towel soaked in cold water or with ice cubes wrapped in a towel.

Traffic Accident Trauma

If a dog is hit by a car, immediately contact a vet and make sure that other drivers become aware of the accident by clearly marking the scene. If necessary, hold the dog in a restraining grip, and carefully check if there are any bleeding wounds before treating the dog for shock. Carefully cover the dog with a coat or blanket and let it lie quietly until you can get it to a vet. It is very important that you do not move the dog unnecessarily, even if no blood or wounds are visible at first sight, as the dog may have suffered internal injuries. You must also therefore avoid giving the dog anything to drink until it has been examined by a vet.

Footpad injury

If your dog is walking awkwardly or licking its paw, there might be a splinter or another object stuck in the sole of its foot. You can carefully remove this with tweezers, disinfect the spot with iodine straight away and bandage it. This prevents the dog licking at the wound and thus infecting it. In the case of heavy blood loss, or if the object is stuck deep in the sole, you need to take your dog to the veterinarian.

Choking

Dogs like to play with all sorts of things, and it is not uncommon for a dog to swallow something by accident. This can result in different consequences ranging from serious to less acute, depending on the size and shape of the object. In the worst case, the swallowed object is stuck just before the windpipe and the dog can no longer breathe -

this is obviously a life-threatening situation. An object, which ends up in the gullet, causes discomfort and sometimes a lot of pain, but the dog is not necessarily in immediate danger. You can recognise when a dog has an object stuck in the gullet by the dog swallowing frequently and trying to throw up. The dog will drool a lot and rub its muzzle. In this case, proceed as follows:

- Hold your dog in a restraining grip if it does not want to accept your help.
- The dog will usually vomit; giving it food or water will only make things worse.
- An object in the gullet is a nuisance, but not life-threatening, therefore remain calm. However, if the object is close to the windpipe, the animal will be in danger, which means that you need to act quickly.
- Open its mouth as far as possible and look into its throat. If the sharp teeth make it difficult to hold the muzzle open, take a dry tissue to carefully pull out the tongue. The dog will keep its mouth open, as it will not risk biting its tongue.
- If the object is clearly visible, you can carefully remove it with tweezers or small pliers. If an object is located just before the windpipe, you can sometimes remove it by putting a finger behind it, deep in the throat. Someone else will have to push on the right spot of the throat from the outside.
- If you do not succeed, lay the dog on its side on a hard surface.
- Apply pressure just behind the last ribs, where the thorax is widest. Push downwards and forwards with both hands, this sometimes makes the object shoot out of the throat.

- Repeat this action several times quickly one after another if you do not succeed the first time. If the object is still stuck in the throat, try removing the object from the throat with your fingers, while someone else continues pressing behind the ribs. If necessary, apply mouth-to-mouth resuscitation.
- If the object has not been removed within a few minutes, take your dog to the veterinarian as quickly as possible. Even if you do manage to remove the object, your vet will still need to examine your dog for possible complications, such as damage to the throat or gullet. Do not take any risks opening the dog's mouth or removing an object - watch your hands and fingers!

Your dog may have swallowed a sharp object, such as a splinter or a fish bone. They will usually get caught in the mucous membranes of the mouth. In this case your dog will rub its muzzle a lot with its paw. It will also salivate excessively, sometimes mixed with blood or retch. Some dogs might sit quietly in one corner, whereas others will run around the house like maniacs.

- Try to have a good look into your dog's throat. If necessary, apply a restraining grip.
- If you have localised the sharp object, you can carefully try to remove it. If it is stuck very tightly, leave it.
- Carefully wipe the froth from the oral cavity and take your dog to the veterinarian as quickly as possible.
- During your journey, hold onto your dog's paws, so that he cannot injure himself by continuously rubbing his muzzle.
- Your vet will remove the object, probably under anaesthetic. After this, your dog will have some problems eating and will need to be fed an adjusted diet.

Wounds

A dog can become wounded in a number of ways. You may therefore encounter a wide range of wounds, which vary in their severity. Roughly, you can divide them into simple wounds, in which only the skin surface has been damaged and complex wounds, in which deeper layers, such as muscles, blood vessels and nerves have also been affected. Both types obviously need to be treated in their own way.
Always take your dog to the veterinarian if it has suffered a severe wound. Graze wounds are best cleaned with warm boiled water.

Modern home hazards

Modern homes are actually a very strange environment for a dog. There are no trees, no grass, and no shrubs and the wind does not blow around their ears. An animal needs to adapt to this domestic setting, and this does not always go smoothly, but you can help make your dog's life with you as safe as possible.

A human walks on two legs and does not always see what can happen at ankle and knee height. You could say that anything that may be dangerous for a crawling baby can also be dangerous for a dog. For example:

Cables

Young dogs like to bite into all sorts of things. Wires from lamps, the computer and other electric appliances can be found everywhere in the house. Hide these where possible, and you can also buy certain materials to wrap around cables to protect them.

Detergents

Although most people do not think of detergents as being immediate hazards for dogs, they contain substances that are toxic. So it stands to reason that you should not let your dog come into contact with detergents. Therefore, it is important to be aware that your dog can ingest toxins from his paws after you have mopped the floor, for example, so exercise extreme caution when using any household cleaning products.

Chocolate

Chocolate is one of those products that humans enjoy, but which is actually toxic for dogs. It contains certain substances that their bodies cannot break down, so never feed a dog chocolate and make sure it isn't left around where your Dobermann can find it.

Avocado

Avocado is also toxic for dogs. It contains persine, which causes serious conditions in dogs.

Onions and garlic

Avoid onions and also garlic, both raw as well as cooked for dogs. It contains a substance that can cause anemia in dogs.

Grapes and raisins

Grapes and raisins are also prohibited for dogs. 30 grams per kilogram of bodyweight is considered toxic and can lead to kidney failure.

Plants

It is common knowledge that dogs sometimes like to eat grass and this, generally, is nothing to be concerned about.

You never know why a dog will take a fancy to a plant, and puppies in particular occasionally like to 'take a bite'. In reality it is unlikely your dog will actually eat a houseplant, but if it does happen, take your dog and a branch of the plant in question to your vet, they will know the best course of action.

On the next pages an overview of toxic home and garden plants is provided.

TOXIC PLANTS

-A-
Abrus precatorius - Precatory-pea
Acer rubrum - Red maple
Aconitum napellus - Monk's hood
Aesculus hippocastanum - Horse chestnut
Ailanthus altissima - Tree-of-heaven
Allamanda cathartica - Golden-trumper
Allium cepa - Onion
Allium sativum - Garlic
Alstroemeria ligtu - Peruvian lily
Amaranthus hybridus - Smooth pigweed
Amaryllis vittata - Amaryllis (*A. vittata*)
Anthurium andraenum - Flamingo lily
Aquilegia alpina - Aquilegia
Asimina triloba - Pawpaw

-B-
Baptista tinctoria - Wild indigo
Barbarea vulgaris - Yellow rocket
Buxus sempervirens - Buxus

-C-
Caladium bicolor - Caladium
Chrysanthemum indicum - Chrysanthemum
Cicuta virosa - Northern water-hemlock
Clematis - Clematis
Clivia miniata - Kaffir lily
Codiaeum variegetum - Croton
Colchicum autumnale - Autumn crocus
Conium macaltum - Poison-hemlock
Convallaria majalis - Lily-of-the-valley
Corydalis - Corydalis
Crocus - Crocus
Cyclamen persicum - Cyclamen

-D-
Dature innoxia - Angel's trumpet
Datura stramonium - Jimsomweed
Delphinium - Larkspur
Dieffenbachia seguine - Mother-in-law-plant
Digitalis purpurea - Foxglove

-E-
Euonymus europaeus - European spindletree
Euphorbia helioscopia - Sun spurge
Euphorbia lacteal - Candelabra-cactus
Euphorbia pulcherrima - Poinsettia

-F-
Fagopyrum esculentem - Tall manna grass

-G-
Gutierrezia sarothrae - Broom snakewood
Gymnocladus dioicus - Kentucky coffeetree

Aquilegia

Buxus

Clematis

Corydalis

Crocus

-H-

Hedera helix - English ivy
Helenium autumnale - Sneezeweed
Helianthus annuus - Sunflower
Heliotropium curassavicum - Spatulate-leaved heliotrope
Heracleum mantegazzianum - Giant hogweed
Humulus lupulus - Common hop
Hyancinthoides nonscripta - English bluebell
Hydrangea macrophylla - Hydrangea
Hypercum perforatum - St. John's wort

-I-

Ilex aquifolium - English holly
Ipomoea tricolour - Morning glory
Iris pseudocorus - Yellow iris
Iris versicolor - Blue flag iris

-J-

Juglans nigra - Black walnut

-K-

Kalanchoe daigremontiana - Devil's-backbone
Kalmia angustofolia - Sheep-laurel

-L-

Laportea canadensus - Canada nettle
Lathyrus odoratus - Sweet pea
Lathyrus sativus - Grass pea
Leonurus cardiaca - Motherwort
Ligistrum vulgare - Common privet
Linaria vulgaris - Yellow toadflax
Lobelia cardinalis - Cardinalflower
Lobelia inflate - Indian-tobacco
Lonicera xylosteum - Fly honeysuckle
Lupinus argenteus - Silvery lupine
Lupinus polyphyllus - Large-leaved lupine
Lupinus pusillus - Small lupine
Lupinus sericeus - Silky lupine

-M-

Mangifera indica - Mango
Medicago sativa - Alfalfa
Melilotus alba - White sweet clover
Melitus officinalis - Yellow sweet clover
Menispermum canadense - Moonseed
Monstera deliciosa - Swiss-cheese plant

-N-

Narcissus peoticus - Narcissus
Narcissus pseudonarcissus - Daffodil
Nerium oleander - Oleander
Nicotiana tabacum - Tobacco

Delphinium

Datura

Digitalis

Euonymus

Hedera

Hydrangea

Ilex

Lonicera

-O-

Onoclea sensibilis - Sensitive fern
Ornithogalum umbellatum - Star-of-Bethlehem
Oxytropus lambertii - Purple locoweed

-P-

Papaver nudicaule - Iceland poppy
Papaver orientale - Oriental poppy
Papaver somniferum - Opium poppy
Parthenocissus quinquefolia - Virginia creeper
Persea americana - Avocado
Phacelia campanularia - California canarygrass
Phalaris arundinacea - Reed canarygrass
Philodendron cordatum - Philodendron
Phoradendron flavescens - American mistletoe
Physalis alkekengi - Chinese-lantern
Physalis peruviana - Ground-cherry
Phytolacca american - Pokeweed
Pinus ponderosa - Ponderosa pine
Primula obconica - Primula
Polygonatum multiflorum - Solomon's seal
Prunus pennsylvanica - Pin cherry
Ptedidium aquilinum - Bracken

-Q-

Quercus alba - White oak
Quercus rubra - Red oak

-R-

Rananculus bulbosus - Bulbous buttercup
Raphanus raphanistrum - Wild radish
Raphanus sativus - Radish
Rhamnus carthartica - European buckthorn
Rheum rhaponticum - Rhubarb
Rhododendron macrophyllum - California rose-baby
Rhus diversiloba - Western poison-oak
Rhus radicans - Poison ivy
Ricinus communis - Castor-bean
Robinia pseudoacacia - Black locust
Rudbeckia serotina - Black-eyed Susan
Rumex acetosa - Garden sorrel

-S-

Sambucus canadensis - American elder
Sambucus nigra - European elder
Sarcobatus vermiculatus - Greasewood
Scilla siberica - Siberian scilla
Senecop jacobaea - Tansy ragwort
Sinapis arvensis - Wild mustard
Solanum dulcamara - Climbing nightshade
Solanum nigrum - Black nightshade
Solanum speudocapsicum - Jerusalem-cherry
Solanum tuberosum - Potato
Solidago mollis - Velvety goldenrod
Sorghum halepense - Johnson Newfoundlands
Suckleya suckleyana - Poison suckleya

Lupinus

Papaver orientalis

Parthenocissus

Phytolacca

Polygonatum Rhododendron

Symphoricarpos albus - Thin-leaved snowberry
Symphytum asperum - Prickly comfrey
Symplocarpus foetidus - Skunk cabbage

-T-
Tanacetum vulgare - Tansy
Taxus canadensis - Canada yew
Thermopsis rhombifolia - Golden-bean
Thlaspi arvense - Stinkweed
Thuja - Thuja
Trifolium pratense - Red clover
Trifolium repens - White clover
Tulipa gesneriana - Tulip

-U-
Urica dioica - Stinging nettle

-V-
Veratrum viride - False hellebore
Viburnum opulus - Guelder-rose
Vicia sativa - Common vetch

-W-
Wisteria floribunda - Japanese wisteria

-X-
Xanthium strumarium - Cocklebur

-Z-
Zigadenus elegans - White camas

Ricinus

Sedum spectabile

Thuja

Tips

- Get in touch with a breed club for the address of a reliable breeder.
- Visit more than one breeder before buying a puppy.
- Ask to see the parent dogs' papers. The parents must not have any hereditary abnormalities such as Hip Dysplasia, hereditary eye conditions nor having a white coat. Furthermore the parents should have had a DNA-test for the "Von Willebrand's Disease".
- Never buy a puppy if you have been unable to see its mother.
- Never buy a Dobermann on impulse.
- The first trip in a car is a real experience for a puppy; make it a pleasant one.
- Do not add supplements to ready-made foods.
- Hard chunks and plenty to chew on keep the teeth healthy.
- Do not let your Dobermann climb up stairs for the first year.
- Join a puppy-training course with your puppy. It teaches both dog and owner a lot.
- Take care that your dog does not get overweight. An appropriate diet and plenty of exercise are golden rules.
- Never leave a dog alone with small children.
- Never let your puppy run endlessly after a ball.
- Do not just fight the fleas, but the larvae too.
- Organise a holiday home or a dog-sitter for your Dobermann well in advance.
- Think carefully before you decide to take your dog on holiday – it may not be the best option for the dog!
- Allow your Dobermann to rest after meals.
- A puppy will mean a lot of work, and sometimes a few grey hairs.
- Good grooming is important for your dog's health.
- Early training is essential to ensure you end up with a well-behaved dog.
- A Dobermann has a strong will, so make sure NO always means NO.
- The Dobermann is a courageous dog full of character, a good upbringing is essential.
- To give your Dobermann enough exercise, it is necessary to make long walks as well as cycle tours (when the dog is old enough). The Dobermann should be able to move next to your bike while he is trotting easily.

Internet

A great deal of further information can be found on the internet. A selection of websites with interesting details and links to other sites and pages are listed here. Sometimes pages move to another site or address. You can find more sites by using the available search engines.

For Great Britain

www.thedobermannclub.co.uk
The Dobermann Club is the national club for the breed in the U.K. The Dobermann Club was established in 1948. The main goals of this national breed club are to foster and promote the interests, welfare and good name of the Dobermann as a working breed.

www.birminghamdobe.co.uk
The Birmingham & District Dobermann Club was formed in the early 70's. In 1979 the Club became a KC recognised training club in 1979 for obedience and ringcraft training. In 1986 the Kennel Club registered the Birmingham Dobermann Club as a Breed Club. On this website you find a lot of information about training, health, shows and more.

www.midland-dobermann-club.co.uk
The Midland Dobermann Club was founded in 1967. On this website you find a lot of interesting information about health issues that affect Dobermanns. Your learn more about the specific disease and you will also find information about check ups etc., the Dobermann Breed Council and information about several events.

www.necds.org.uk
The North Eastern Counties Dobermann Society was founded in 1986. Health, shows and training are the issues that can be found on this website.

www.nedc.me.uk
The North of England Dobermann Club was founded in 1964. This club is happy to provide all information concerning Dobermann matters. Apart from that the club offers educational seminars and shows. Information about several health projects can be found, and addresses for Rescue and Rehoming Dobermanns.

www.scottishdobermannclub.com
The Scottish Dobermann Club promotes Scottish Dobermanns all over the world. In the website you find information about social events, shows-results, training tips, breeders pages and more.

www.seedc.co.uk
The South East of England Dobermann Club was recognised by the Kennel Club in March 1987. This club offers lots of events and information about health concerns within the breed.

www.southwestdobermannclub.co.uk
The South West Dobermann Club was formed in spring 1986.
There is interesting information about health concerns, where the symptoms and the possible treatment are very well described.

www.welshdobermann.co.uk
The Welsh Dobermann Club exists since 1969. You find a rescue page, articles about the Dangerous Dog Act, information about the huge health problems with the Albino Dobermann and other health conditions.

Dog related websites

www.the-kennel-club.org.uk
The Kennel Club's primary objective is to promote, in every way, the general improvement of dogs. This site aims to provide you with information you may need to be a responsible pet owner and to help you keep your dog happy, safe and content.

www.crufts.org.uk
Welcome to the website of dfs Crufts. The Crufts is the world's largest dog show!

www.discoverdogs.org.uk
Discover Dogs is London's biggest event on four legs, and it is meant for families, kids and dogs. On this event every participant has a great time while celebrating all things positive about man's best friend. This event is organised by the British Kennel Club.

www.k9-care.co.uk
The Self-Help site for dog owners. A beautiful website with tons of information on dogs. All you need to know about grooming, training, health care, buying a dog, travel and much more.

www.doggenetichealth.org
Your one stop resource for practical information and to learn about dog genetic health. A guide for dog breeders and owners, brought to you by The Kennel Club.

www.thedogscene.co.uk
This website is run by dog lovers for dog lovers in the UK. Their primary purpose is to spread the word about responsible dog ownership and dog breeding. They provide you with all the help and information and the right contacts that you need to have a happy, healthy relationship with your dog. The Dog Scene provides a lot of information concerning dogs, and more is being added all the time.

For U.S.A.

www.akc.org
The website of the American Kennel Club, with lots and lots of information. The AKC provides coverage on all accepted breeds. Gives information on registration, pedigrees and dog shows. Look at the website! So much to see about breeders, breeds, registration, addresses and events.

www.ukcdogs.com
The website of the United Kennel Club, this club was established in 1998. It is the largest all-breed performance-dog registry in the world, registering dogs from all 50 states and 25 foreign countries.

www.dpca.org/
The Dobermann Pinscher Club of America is the national club and founded in 1921. This website offers the visitor a wide range of interesting information such as: History of the breed, health, colour inheritance, albino Dobermanns and their problems, education, shows and much more.
You also find a page about DCPA Rescue Dogs.

www.aboutpets.info
The website of the publisher of the About Pets book series. An overview of the titles, availability in which languages and where in the world the books are sold.

Addresses

Becoming a member of a breed club can be very useful for good advice and interesting activities. A Dobermann club will give you the opportunity to meet other Dobermann lovers. Contact The Kennel Club in case addresses or telephone numbers have changed.

The Kennel Club
1 - 5 Clarges Street
Piccadilly
London WIJ 8AB
Tel.: 0870 606 6750
Fax: 020 7518 1058
www.thekennelclub.org.uk

Scottish Kennel Club
Eskmills Park Station Road Musselburgh
Edinburgh EH21 7PQ
Tel.: 0131 665 3920
Fax: 0131 653 6937
www.scottishkennelclub.org
E-mail: info@scottishkennelclub.org

The Irish Kennel Club
Fottrell House, Harrolds Cross Bridge,
Dublin 6W, Ireland
Tel.: +353 (1) 4533 300,
+353 (1) 4532 309
+353 (1) 4532 309
Fax: +353 (1) 4533 237
www.ikc.ie
E-mail: ikenclub@indigo.ie

Dobermann Club (National Club)
www.thedobermannclub.co.uk
E-mail: vivluc@aol.com

Birmingham & District Dobermann Club
www.birminghamdobe.co.uk
E-mail: von.zeloviak@btconnect.com

Midland Dobermann Club
www.midland-dobermann-club.co.uk
E-mail: remesca@aol.com

North Eastern Counties Dobermann Society
www.necds.org.uk
E-mail: alison.richardson3@btopenworld.com

North Of England Dobermann Club
www.nedc.me.uk
E-mail: wendy.meikle@ntlworld.com

Northern Ireland Dobermann Club
No website nor E-mail available
Secr.: Mr. S. Richardson
Phone: 07711 – 77 92 29

Pennine Dog Training Club
No website available
Secr.: Mrs. J. K. Knott
E-mail: karen.knott@tesco.net

Scottish Dobermann Club
www.scottishdobermannclub.com
E-mail: tracy@diegodobermanns.freeserve.co.uk

South East Of England Dobermann Club
www.seedc.co.uk
E-mail: janeandrodney@tiscali.co.uk

South West Dobermann Club
www.southwestdobermannclub.co.uk
E-mail: sylvia@philmont.freeserve.co.uk

Welsh Dobermann Club
www.welshdobermannclub.co.uk
E-mail: junewelshdobie@btinternet.com

Dobermann Rehoming Association
Mrs. Chris Omar
Phone: 01276 – 85 53 26

Rescue / Rehoming Groups Dobermann Welfare
Treasurer and Rehoming Coordinator
Sue Garner
E-mail: sue.garner@ca.com
Phone: 01895 – 25 35 78

For U.S.A.

American Kennel Club
A.K.C. Customer Care
8051 Arco Corporate Drive, Suite 100
Raleigh, NC 27617-3390
Tel.: 00 1 919 233 9767 from 08:30 until 17.00 o'clock weekdays (Monday - Friday) except holidays
www.akc.org

U.K.C.
100 E Kilgore Rd Kalamazoo
MI 49002 – 5584
Office hours: 09:00 to 16:30 (E.S.T.)
Monday through Friday.
Tel.: 269 – 343 – 9020
Fax: 269 – 343 – 7037
www.ukcdogs.com

Breed Association

Dobermann Pinscher Club of America
www.dpca.org
E-mail: DPCAcorrespondingsecretary@dpca.org

Profile

Name in the U.K.: Dobermann

Name in the U.S.A.: Dobermann Pinscher

KC Group U.K.: Working Group

A.K.C. Group: Working Group

F.C.I. Classification: Group 2: Pinchers and Schnauzers, Molossers and Swiss mountain dogs
Section 1: Pinscher and Schnauzer type, with working trial

FCI-Standard N°: 143 /14. 02. 1994 / GB

Origin: Germany

Breed Association established:
On 27th August 1899 the first club of this breed was established, the Dobermann Pinscher Club Apolda in Germany. Several years later this club was called 'Urklub von 1899' (Original club from 1899). One year later, 1900, the name was changed into Nationaler Dobermann Pinscher Klub für Deutschland e.V. In 1921 the first American Dobermann Pinscher Club was established. In the U.K. 'The Dobermann Club' is the national club for the breed, and was established in 1948.

First breed standard: 1899
In the UK, the Kennel Club recognized the Dobermann Pinscher in 1951.
The A.K.C. registered the first Dobermann Pinscher in 1908.

Original use: Watch and guard dog

Use today: Companion, protection and working dog

Height at withers: UK Kennel Club: Ideal height at withers for dogs: 69 cms (27 ins) and for bitches: 65 cms (251/2 ins). Considerable deviation from this ideal undesirable.

AKC: Height at withers for dogs 26 to 28 inches, ideal about 27½ inches. For bitches 24 to 26 inches, ideal about 25½ inches.

Life expectancy (average): 10 to 12 years